CW01456932

Time of Death

Time of Death: A Sociological Exploration

BY

GLENYS CASWELL

Independent Social Researcher, UK

emerald
PUBLISHING

United Kingdom – North America – Japan – India – Malaysia – China

Emerald Publishing Limited
Emerald Publishing, Floor 5, Northspring, 21-23 Wellington Street, Leeds LS1 4DL

First edition 2024

Copyright © 2024 Glenys Caswell.
Published under exclusive licence by Emerald Publishing Limited.

Reprints and permissions service
Contact: www.copyright.com

No part of this book may be reproduced, stored in a retrieval system, transmitted in any form or by any means electronic, mechanical, photocopying, recording or otherwise without either the prior written permission of the publisher or a licence permitting restricted copying issued in the UK by The Copyright Licensing Agency and in the USA by The Copyright Clearance Center. Any opinions expressed in the chapters are those of the authors. Whilst Emerald makes every effort to ensure the quality and accuracy of its content, Emerald makes no representation implied or otherwise, as to the chapters' suitability and application and disclaims any warranties, express or implied, to their use.

British Library Cataloguing in Publication Data
A catalogue record for this book is available from the British Library

ISBN: 978-1-80455-006-9 (Print)
ISBN: 978-1-80455-005-2 (Online)
ISBN: 978-1-80455-007-6 (Epub)

Printed and bound by CPI Group (UK) Ltd, Croydon, CR0 4YY

INVESTOR IN PEOPLE

To Alan for your care, support and belief during the writing of this book.

Contents

List of Abbreviations

A&E	Accident & Emergency
AMRC	Academy of Medical Royal Colleges
APT	Anatomical Pathology Technologist
BCE	Before the Common Era
BMA	British Medical Association
CCTV	Closed Circuit Television
CE	Common Era
ICD	International Classification of Diseases
ICRC	International Committee of the Red Cross
NIIS	National Health Service (UK)
ONS	Office for National Statistics (UK)
RSPB	Royal Society for the Protection of Birds
UK	United Kingdom (of Great Britain and Northern Ireland)
UN	United Nations
WHO	World Health Organization

About the Author

Glenys Caswell is an independent death studies scholar and University of Nottingham associate. She is a sociologist by training and her area of research interest focuses on the social management of dying and death. She has researched and published on aspects of dying alone, time of death and Scottish funerals. This is her second book, the first being called *Dying Alone: Challenging Assumptions*, which was published in 2022.

Preface

In 2017, I gave a paper at the 13th International Conference on the Social Context of Death, Dying and Bereavement, which took place at the University of Central Lancashire, in Preston in the north of England. The paper focused on the ways in which dying alone was represented in the media, and one person attending suggested that time would make an interesting lens through which to look at experiences and representations of dying alone. This seemed so obvious that I wondered how I could not have thought of it myself. It also prompted me to think about death and dying more broadly in terms of time. It also led me to think about the time when my mother died and to realise that although I knew she died in May 1999, I could not remember the date nor the time of day. And I also realised that it didn't matter. I remembered, instead, the overall experience which was one of a gathering of family. I searched the academic literature for research and thinking about time in relation to death. I found swathes of work on time, including in the social sciences, but not so much about time in relation to death. As someone who enjoys detective stories for the narrative tendency to tie up all the loose ends and restore order to a chaotic world, I began to look into how true to life fictional pathologists are when they state confidently when someone died. By following up on the ideas, theories and stories about time that I found, I fell down the proverbial rabbit hole and, realising that I had no idea what time actually is, I felt compelled to do some explorations of my own. This is the first outcome of that work.

Acknowledgements

There are a number of people and organisations to whom I owe thanks, as I would not have been able to write this book without their different contributions. First, I would like to thank the British Academy and the Leverhulme Trust for funding the research on which the book relies in constructing its argument. I would also like to say thank you to Katy Mathers and the team at Emerald for their supportive approach while I was writing the book. Most important of all, I want to say a sincere thank you to Home Office registered forensic pathologist, Dr Stuart Hamilton, and to all the people who took part in my research. I appreciate your generosity in sharing your knowledge, time and experiences with me, and I can truly say that without you there would have been no book. So thank you.

Chapter 1

Introduction

Agatha Christie's novel, *The Murder of Roger Ackroyd*, was first published in 1926. In the book, Roger Ackroyd is a wealthy man who lives in a big house with members of his family as well as servants. In the story, he is murdered while in his study, and his body is left there while the murderer, Dr Sheppard, subverts time in an effort to escape detection. Dr Sheppard is the local general practitioner and he also has an interest in tinkering with contemporary technology, such as alarm clocks and recording devices. He makes a recording of Roger Ackroyd speaking on a dictaphone. Sheppard then kills Ackroyd, sets the recording to play at a certain time and leaves the body in the study where, he tells the butler as he leaves the house, Mr Ackroyd has said that he is not to be disturbed. Sheppard then goes home, and he arranges for a phone call to be made to his house later that day which makes it seem as if he has been summoned to Ackroyd's home, in his capacity as doctor. This means that he is on hand when the corpse is discovered and he is able to hide the dictaphone in his medical bag, before anyone else can see it. Dr Sheppard has established for himself an alibi, for witnesses who were in the house can attest that they know Roger Ackroyd was alive after the murderer left the house because they heard him speaking. The murderer appeared to be getting away with his crime but, unfortunately for him, Christie's Belgian detective, Hercule Poirot, had moved into the village when he retired and he was able to solve the murder when the local police force could not (Christie, 1926/2007).

Sheppard subverts time, for no one can be in two places at one time, but Poirot reasserts time and reveals what Sheppard has done (Sandberg, 2022). A century later, Sheppard's actions still make sense to readers. Detective stories continue to be popular, in the form of novels, stage plays, films and television programmes. They often hinge upon the alibis which suspects have, or appear to have, at the time when the murder is believed to have been committed. The technologies involved might be different, but 21st century fictional murderers may also attempt to subvert time in an effort to escape punishment, and consumers of such literature understand the requirements of the genre.

The expectation for readers of fictional murders is that the time at which the victim is murdered will become clear, even if at first it is obscure. The work of the forensic scientists and the pathologist will combine to elucidate the details of how

Time of Death, 1–10
Copyright © 2024 Glenys Caswell
Published under exclusive licence by Emerald Publishing Limited
doi:10.1108/978-1-80455-005-220241001

and when the killing took place; that is, the time of death will be described with a date on the calendar and a time on the clock. But this is fiction and, generally speaking, readers and viewers expect a tidy resolution to the case, suggesting that perhaps sometimes the world can be a place where justice prevails and loose ends tie together nicely.

However, in the world where we live our daily lives things are often messy and confused, and time of death as a concept is no exception. This book, therefore, tells a mystery story about the time of death and, unlike most fictional murder mysteries, there is no clear answer at the end. Instead, the book argues that time of death is not the straightforward concept we might assume. Time is embedded in our individual and collective consciousness, as the operation of 21st century society depends upon timing and synchronisation. We know what time is and how it works, even if we are unable to define what it is. And death is similar. We know that every living creature must die, even if we dislike thinking about it, and we know this applies to humans, too. We know what death means, we understand that the person is no longer with us and will not be coming back, we have been to their funeral and escorted them on the start of their final journey. So time of death must mean the moment when a person ceases to exist. But when does an individual cease to exist? Is that the moment when their body stops functioning, the moment when they cease to have social relevance or when we stop thinking about them and taking them into account in our lives? Or is it some other, completely different, time?

Core Argument

The central argument of this book is that time of death is a social construction, and one which is context dependent. It will explore whether it is possible to identify and record the date and time of an individual's death using the calendar and clock. Throughout the book, the question, 'when is the time of death?' is asked, suggesting that it is necessary to understand the context within which the question is being asked to be able to give a meaningful answer. The answer will vary according to the particular set of circumstances within which the individual responding to the query is situated. For example, if the question is asked of bereaved people whose close person has died in 21st century United Kingdom, the response is likely to be different from that given by a medical professional whose responsibility it is to either verify or certify a death.

Time is a concept which individuals and groups use to organise their experiences as they go through their lives, and this includes the period when they must engage with experiences of dying, death and bereavement. Every human goes through two deaths, which are the death of their body and their social death. Each death is a process, not a one off, momentary event. This complicates the way in which a time of death can be assigned, raising questions about what point in the process of dying should be assigned a time and how that time should be constituted.

The time of death concept seems to be straightforward when we speak of it, but the book will show that this is far from accurate. How people in a social setting think about the time of death as a concept is dependent upon their perceptions of both time and death. While different societies have differing views on these issues, time of death is important to individuals. Years of birth and death are commonly recorded on gravestones, while obituaries regularly include dates of birth and death, as well as age at death. The time of some deaths shock many people and reverberate down the decades, such as that of the Reverend Dr Martin Luther King who was shot dead at a time recorded as 6:05 p.m. on Thursday, 4 April 1968.[1] The impact which Dr King's death had, and the memorability of when he died, comes from the significance of the role which he played in the American civil rights movement and what an important figure he was internationally, both during his lifetime and today. We recall, perhaps, the time of death of people who are important to us when we have close emotional and personal ties to them, and we may also do so when the significance of the individual is at one remove and we have never met the deceased person. Historically, family, friends and kin attended the deathbed of a dying person as witness to this significant moment and this practice continues into the 21st century (Caswell et al., 2022).

There is much about the time of death which requires investigation. The taken for granted understandings that we have of time, that it is what is shown upon the clock face and the notion that time is something which flows unidirectionally from the past and into the future, require challenge. The idea that time does not always behave in an expected manner, given the regularity of clocks and calendars, is acknowledged by all competent users of time, yet the ways in which individuals experience the passage of time when they, or someone about whom they care, is dying have been little researched. The ways in which time and death link together, particularly in relation to time of death, is an under explored field of enquiry for social scientists. This book is intended to make a contribution to that field of endeavour.

Conceptual Background

People are surrounded by death. The leaves on deciduous trees turn brown in the autumn and fall from the tree, annual plants die at the end of their growing season and cut flowers begin the process of dying once they are removed from the parent plant. This is all part of the natural order and it does not appear to trouble humans very much. Even in the animal kingdom death is a familiar sight. Animals are killed for meat in many human diets and cuts of meat are put on view in butcher's shops and supermarkets. Foxes, badgers and hedgehogs can be seen dead at the side of the road, having fallen prey to motor vehicles, our cats sometimes bring us the birds and mice that they kill as presents, and we have to

---

[1]Stanford University, Martin Luther King Jr Research Institute, 'Assassination of Martin Luther King, Jr'. https://kinginstitute.stanford.edu/encyclopedia/assassination-martin-luther-king-jr

deal with the deaths of our children's treasured pet rabbit, hamster or goldfish. The deaths of other people are also a staple of the media and entertainment industries, with news reports about wars and murders alongside a wide variety of cultural representations of both fictional and non-fictional deaths (Caswell, 2020).

The fact of death in the abstract is familiar to anyone who is at all observant of the world around them, but it is doubtful whether this knowledge is transferred to people's own particular situations. We do know that we must die, if we allow ourselves to acknowledge this, but fear of death may act as preventive mechanism and stop us considering our own mortality and eventual death (Menzies & Menzies, 2021).

What is regarded in any social setting as an appropriate time and manner of dying is dependent upon context. In the United Kingdom, for example, historically it was children who experienced a high mortality rate and they frequently died from an infectious disease (Doig, 2022). Overall, life expectancy in previous centuries was shorter than it is in the 21st century and people tended to become ill and die in the home where they lived, cared for by family members. Much has changed, so that today when children and young people die we say that they have been taken too soon, for it is older people who are most represented among the annual death statistics. In 2021, for example, in England and Wales, 852 deaths of children aged between one and 15 years were registered, representing a mortality rate of 8 deaths per 100,000 of population (Office for National Statistics, 2023). This is within a context where approximately 90% of all deaths take place among people aged 60 and over (Office for National Statistics, 2014).

Life expectancy in the United Kingdom, as in other privileged societies, is much extended, especially for the more affluent members of society. In contrast, it is estimated that approximately 741 homeless people died in England and Wales during 2021. For homeless men, the average age at death was 45.4 years and for women it was 43.2 years (Office for National Statistics, 2022a). This compares unfavourably with the age at death of the general population, which is about 74 for men and 80 for women, so being homeless takes over 30 years off a person's life expectancy (Webb et al., 2020). The most common causes of death have also changed and individuals in the United Kingdom are more likely to die from cancer, cardiac or respiratory disease in the 21st century than they are to die from an infectious disease (Ritchie et al., 2019).[2]

Proverbially speaking, death has been described as the 'great leveller' for, as in James Shirley's poem, *Death the Leveller*, everyone must die whether they are a prince or a pauper.[3] That is true, of course, but only in the sense that death is inevitable for everyone. It is in the when and the how that inequalities in life become inequalities in death, as can be observed with the reduced life expectancy of people experiencing homelessness (Salisbury, 2022).

---

[2]This does not take deaths from COVID-19 into account during the period of the global pandemic which began in 2020, when greater numbers of people than usual died from an infectious disease. For information on the numbers of people who have died globally see the WHO Coronavirus (COVID-19) Dashboard: https://covid19.who.int/ For UK figures on deaths from COVID-19 see: https://coronavirus.data.gov.uk/details/deaths
[3]Bartleby.com, James Shirley, 1596–1666, Death the Leveller: https://www.bartleby.com/101/288.html

Everyone, however, has to deal with the fact that they will die, whether they are in a privileged position or not, for ignore it as they wish, ultimately death will catch up with them when the time comes for their personal appointment in Samarra (Maugham, 1933/2017). It is also the case that along the way in their life they will need to deal with the deaths of other people. Some of the people they will not know personally, but some they will, perhaps as acquaintances or colleagues, and there will be others who die to whom they are close and whose deaths will leave them feeling bereft.

The lives of all living creatures are bounded by time, they have a beginning and an end, however long or short their lifespan may be. Time in the global north[4] is conceived as being linear, running from the past, through the present and into the future, but other ways of perceiving the passage of time are possible. For example, some cultures see time as being cyclical, which resonates with the turn of the seasons and the ways in which the dead bodies of plants and animals return to the earth through decomposition (Baggini, 2018). Death comes for an individual human when they reach the end of their life as an embodied person. It only seems possible to make sense of one's own death and the deaths of other humans by reference to time. This, however, leads to questions about the nature of time, whether it exists and what it is or might be. Time is embedded not only in human dying and death but also in our living and lives. Take a moment before you read on to think about how you would define time, and whether you are like theologian and philosopher St. Augustine of Hippo, who wrote that he knew what time was until he tried to explain it to someone else (Hernandez, 2016).

The very familiarity and everydayness of time make it seem obvious and uncomplicated, yet there is a long history of thinkers grappling with time, its nature, questions about its existence and how to measure it. From the days of Ancient Greece onwards, physicists, astronomers, philosophers, social scientists, creative writers, scholars of religion and humanities and more have all addressed different aspects of time and temporality (Clark, 2023; de Jong, 2007).

Humans use time as a means of organising their life experiences, relating them to each other in a more or less coherent story (Sacks, 2015). The use of chronology, placing events in the temporal order in which they occurred, is for some a useful way of trying to make sense of events which appear confusing. Putting together a timeline or telling a story from the beginning through to the end can be helpful, as some things simply do not make sense if they are not in the correct chronological order. Take, for example, the famous comedy sketch by Eric Morecambe and Ernie Wise, first shown on British television in 1971. In it the world famous conductor, André Previn, joined them to conduct the orchestra playing Grieg's piano concerto in A minor. Eric Morecambe was to be the solo pianist, and the sketch was intended to be funny, but the piano playing sounded wrong. This led to queries from Previn and the riposte from Morecambe that, 'I'm playing all the right notes, but not necessarily in the right

---

[4]The terms global south and global north are used here as shorthand ways of referring to countries which have lesser or greater access to the world's resources. The choice to use such terminology is not straightforward and is not intended to imply any form of judgement. See Horner and Carmody (2020) for a discussion of some of the issues involved.

order'. As comedy it made sense, because both the audience in the studio and those watching on television at home knew that for music to be comprehensible all the notes must be in the right order, and these notes were definitely not in the right order.[5] Life events often only seem to make sense when they are experienced and placed in the right temporal order, just like the notes of Grieg's piano concerto.

Time is important, too, in the context of people's understanding of their own lives. One theory suggests that individuals construct a narrative of their lives, telling themselves their own story which situates them within their personal and social context, and which uses their memories of the past to anchor them in the present. The belief is that this story defines the person (Sacks, 2015). The universality of this theory is not without its challengers, however (Strawson, 2015), although it does highlight that people live with, in and through time and that they lack choice in the matter, for it is difficult to remove time from our lives. Time is not just the backdrop to human lives but a constituent factor and an agent in the production of social life (Bastion et al., 2020).

Despite the difficulty in defining what time is, in their daily lives people know how it works. They understand how to use clocks and calendars and all that is involved in scheduling activities of all kinds. They also understand that there are occasions when it will seem to them as if time is not moving in its usual linear fashion but is passing more slowly or swiftly than normal. Given the ubiquity of time and its embeddedness in human lives, it is impossible to remove it from experiences of dying and death because they are part of the life and living of which time is a key constituent.

The Research Studies

The core argument of the book, that the time of death is a social construction which is contextually dependent, will be presented and supported using three different kinds of evidence. First, a wide range of literature will be drawn upon from differing academic disciplines, as well as from outside the academy. This will mainly focus on what is directly relevant and already known, as it aids discussion of the topic. Second, data from an interview with a forensic pathologist will be drawn on. This interview was conducted outside a formal research project and with the specific intention of informing the writing of this book. The third form of data come from two research studies and these are introduced here.

Study 1: Exploring Social Understandings of Time of Death

This was a qualitative research study, funded by the British Academy, which ran between November 2019 and March 2021. Its focus was specifically on the concept of

---

[5]Graham McCann, 2020, Comedy Chronicles, The Prelude of Mr Preview: How André Previn won over Morecambe & Wise: https://www.comedy.co.uk/features/comedy_chronicles/andre-previn-prelude-preview/
Clip from the show: https://www.youtube.com/watch?v=uMPEUcVyJsc

the time of death. The aim of the study was to explore how bereaved people and professionals working in relevant spheres experienced and understood the time of death. The original intention had been to conduct face to face interviews with participants, but by the time ethical approval was received from the University of Nottingham Faculty of Medicine and Health Sciences Research Ethics Committee COVID-19 restrictions were in place. Interviews were therefore carried out either online or by phone, whichever the participant preferred. Semi-structured interviews were used to generate data and these were audio-recorded with participants' permission. Recordings were transcribed by a professional transcriptionist to aid analysis. Analysis was carried out with NVivo© as a data management tool and using the constant comparative approach in order to ground the findings in the data (Charmaz, 2006).

Bereaved participants were sought by advertising in a free monthly newsletter which was delivered to all homes in one postcode area; if anyone was interested in taking part or in learning more they could contact the researcher direct. Twenty people got in touch to enquire about the project, resulting in 17 interviews with bereaved individuals. Five professionals took part in interviews, recruited through social media or through an organisation with which they were involved. Further information about participants will be found in Chapters 5 and 6. In the text, professionals are referred to by their job role, and bereaved participants have been given pseudonyms in order to protect their anonymity.

Overview of Findings

Time as it is measured by the clock still existed for the bereaved participants, but it moved differently. Some participants were not at all aware of time, while others felt its difference for they were outside normal time parameters. Time was effectively suspended in an expanded present (Baraitser, 2017). The moment of dying is important, and most participants wished to be with their dying person at that moment and to be aware of it. This dying moment, however, was within and was part of the expanded present, which was made up of the period when their person was dying, the time at which they died and the immediate aftermath of the death, before their future began without the embodied presence of their person. Time was suspended for participants not so much in the sense that it stopped passing as they all knew that time continued to run, just as they all knew that their person had died; but for a period, time ceased to have relevance or importance.

Professionals working with people who are dying and with the bodies of those who have died experienced time in a different way from those who had been bereaved. For professionals, there tended to be responsibilities which had time implications and required them to pay attention to clock time. For example, the palliative care nurse was aware of guidelines outlining time limits within which the deaths of her patients should be verified and certified. The funeral director also had temporal responsibilities, including the need to embalm bodies as soon as possible after death, in an effort to delay the effects of decomposition so that families could view the body of their person.

Study 2: Exploring the Social Management of Lone Deaths

This was a study which ran between 2018 and 2020 in England and Wales, funded by the Leverhulme Trust. Findings from this study and full details of the methods involved have been reported elsewhere (Caswell, 2022). The study used a range of methods, including the compilation of case studies, documentary analysis, interviews and observations. For this book, only one component of the research is drawn upon, and that is the set of 10 case studies that were established (Yin, 2009). These case studies were of people who lived alone, and then died while alone at home and whose bodies were undiscovered for an extended period of time which ranged from a couple of days to several years. The compilation of each case study began with the coroner's file on the death. When someone dies in England and Wales and there is doubt as to the identity of the person or the cause of death, or there is the possibility of third party involvement in their death, then it must be reported to the coroner who will oversee the enquiry if they deem one to be necessary (Dorries, 2014). In the case of deaths when a person dies alone at home in the way described here, the police will examine the home to ensure that there has been no one else involved in the death and there will be a post-mortem examination to exclude the possibility of homicide. The coroner's file thus includes police reports, post-mortem reports and witness statements, a report from the person's general practitioner, as well as the coroner's own report of the findings and the outcome.

This file was the starting point for exploring the circumstances in which the person lived and died. Other documents were added to the case, such as media coverage when there was any. Efforts were made to talk to somebody who had known the person, and a sister, a brother and a friend of three different individuals were interviewed. An interview was also carried out with a police officer who had been first on the scene in one of the cases. Data from some of the case studies will be referenced, particularly in Chapter 5.

As with study 1, ethical approval was given by the University of Nottingham Faculty of Medicine and Health Sciences ethics committee. There were, however, particular ethical issues at play in this research project. The most resonant here is that the individuals who formed the subjects of the 10 case studies were all dead before the research began, so that there was no possibility of them consenting to participation. The ways in which they lived and died were such that making individuals identifiable in any publications could lead to the criticism of their life choices, assumptions being made about them and attention being drawn to them as individuals when they had lived private lives (Turner & Caswell, 2020). The decision was thus made to protect individuals' identities through the use of pseudonyms and by changing minor details without altering their story (Caswell & Turner, 2020).

Outline of the Book

There are a further 7 chapters in the book which, collectively, will put forward and support the book's argument as it has been outlined here. To begin to make any sense of the concept time of death, it will be necessary to explore each concept separately before examining how they link together. Each chapter thus has its own role to play, as detailed below.

Chapter 2 focuses on the topic of time and asks the question 'what is time?' It draws on a wide range of literature to explore some ideas about what time is and whether or not it has an objective existence outside the human mind. It suggests that societies and their members know what time is through living and experiencing it. It explores ways in which time has been and is measured and considers some of the ways in which people experience time. It concludes with the claim that time is a social construction and lays out some of the constructs which will be used in the examination of the concept 'time of death'.

Chapter 3 turns the focus onto death. On first consideration this may seem to be a straightforward topic, but closer thought will reveal that this is not the case at all. Humans are aware that all living creatures will die, and this awareness can create feelings of anxiety or denial which may lead to attempts to stave off the time of death or even eliminate the possibility of dying. This chapter thinks about the death of the body and how definitions of this have changed over time and place. It also considers social death, and the ways in which individuals can be treated as if already dead when they are still biologically alive, or as if they are still alive after their body has died. The suggestion is made here that each person dies twice, once when their body dies and once when they cease to exist as a social being. Death is a process of change which occurs when a person is on a trajectory of dying and change continues after their bodily death through processes of decomposition and the lessening of their social impact.

Chapter 4 takes on the task of bringing time and death together. It looks at time as a concept which people use to organise their experiences around death and dying, and the role of time in the awareness of mortality that people have. It reviews what is already known about how people who are approaching the end of their lives experience time, and time in relation to both bodily and social death. The chapter proposes that people who are involved in a death, whether as the dying person or as someone who is being, or has been, bereaved is likely to be living in a liminal time, an in between time (Turner, 1969). It then discusses the time of death as a social construction, ready for the following two chapters which present the data.

Chapter 5 offers a problematisation of the ways of and motivations for measuring time of death, by drawing on both the literature and empirical data. It notes how, in the 19th century, the countries which now make up the United Kingdom began to record the deaths of people which occurred within their borders in a more systematic way. This set in place a system for monitoring deaths and their causes which, in the 21st century, is part of the official state statistical organisation. The way in which each death must be legally certified has led to a process whereby the official date of death is the date of certification, not the date when the person died. Data from study 1 and study 2 are drawn upon to highlight anomalies in the way that dates of deaths are recorded. The chapter also highlights issues of power which are inherent in the temporal measuring of death.

Chapter 6 focuses on the ways in which the time at which a person dies is experienced by those who are emotionally close to them, by drawing on empirical data from study 1. Most research participants said that they had not thought about their experience in terms of time, yet they were temporally sophisticated enough to be able to participate in meaningful dialogue about their experience. The chapter suggests a number of temporal constructs to assist in understanding participants' experiences around the time of death and concludes that those experiences are too complex to be limited to explanation by reference to time on a clock and a calendar.

Chapter 7 draws on data and discussions from the previous chapters in order to think about the social construction of time in relation to death in a little more depth. It notes how death is contextually dependent and again separates out bodily death from social death. It outlines the different ways in which people die and the temporal constructs that aid in making sense of them.

Chapter 8 is a short concluding chapter which considers the issue of time of death from two perspectives that of the institutions involved, such as the state and the legal profession, and that of the individuals who experience a death. It reviews some of the factors which need to be taken into account when assigning a time of death in a specific case, and discusses whether it would matter to the way in which we live and die, should it turn out that time does not exist. The chapter ends by considering why this is an important topic to explore and why it is that social sciences have a key role in that exploration.

Closing Thoughts

This book deals with a real-life, non-fiction, mystery story. It attempts to bring together the concepts of time and death, which are each mysterious in their own way, in an effort to enhance understanding of what it means to talk about the time of death. The case is made here that time of death is an important topic to address and one to which sociology is well placed to make a useful contribution. What time is, and what time of death is, are both routinely taken for granted. In keeping with its role as a sociological text, this book questions some of the assumptions which underpin the taken for granted nature of time of death. It begins the process by asking questions about what time is.

Chapter 2

A Brief Look at Time

Introduction

There is an array of literature on the topic of time, from academic work across a range of disciplines to literature, including novels, poetry and drama, which addresses the topic of time from many different perspectives. This seems to suggest that time is an important topic for humans and also that there is a great deal to say about it. The purpose of this chapter is to think about time and reflect on what it is, utilising a small fraction of that literature. In doing so, this chapter will, along with Chapters 3 and 4, begin to set out the temporal constructs which will inform the ensuing discussion in Chapters 5 and 6 about time of death. It will approach the concept of time as being something of a mystery (Rovelli, 2017). Humans know what time is through living and experiencing it, rather than through objective knowledge, and it is this subjective understanding which is key to the exploration of time of death. The idea that we do not know what time is, may appear to be troubling, but it need not be, for '...doubt is not to be feared, but welcomed and discussed...' (Feynman, 1955, p. 15); uncertainty is a normal aspect of the human condition (Honkasalo, 2006).

The chapter begins with a brief exploration of the mystery of time, drawing on a number of different disciplines, to consider what we do know about time and its nature. This will be followed by a section looking at the methods we use to measure time, and how its measurement gives an appearance of time being under human control. The next part of the chapter is concerned with human perceptions of time, particularly with the notion that time is either linear or cyclical in nature. In whatever way people perceive time, it is often the case that we experience it in different ways in different situations, and often as neither linear nor cyclical. Several different ways of experiencing time will therefore be considered, with an emphasis on those which contribute to the book's central argument about the time of death.

The Mystery of Time

The simplest way in which to answer the question about what time is, is to acknowledge that we do not know. After centuries of debate on the part of some

Time of Death, 11–28
Copyright © 2024 Glenys Caswell
Published under exclusive licence by Emerald Publishing Limited
doi:10.1108/978-1-80455-005-220241002

of the world's greatest thinkers, the nature of time, or even whether it exists, remains a mystery (Baron et al., 2022; Rovelli, 2017; Schweizer, 2008). It remains an important question to ask, however, because time is pervasive throughout people's lives and their deaths, and it has a taken for granted quality which often prevents us from questioning what time is or is not. The ways in which humans perceive and think about time, the assumptions we make about its existence and its nature suggest that without time and its apparent effects, our lives would be in stasis and there would be no change, no development, we would simply be. Yet experience indicates the reverse; human lives are not in stasis but are subject to continual forces of change and movement.

However, there is more than one way of accounting for the lack of stasis and the sense which humans have of time's reality and its passage. For example, the philosopher Young (2022) suggests that the sense of passing time may come from within the human brain and the way in which it makes sense of the continual churn of ideas, actions, movements and thoughts. This gives us a sense that the world outside us is subject to the flow of time, but Young argues that it is possible that we are in the process of movement and change and that '(T)he feeling of time passing is the feeling of acting, of effecting change' (Young, 2022, p. 2635).

Sophisticated ways of measuring time with clocks and calendars have been developed, but human knowledge and experience of time involves much more than its measurement. Physics, astronomy and philosophy, among other disciplines, have endeavoured to develop understanding of what time is and how it works. The social sciences, arts, humanities and psychology have, on the other hand, explored the myriad ways in which people experience and understand time in their daily lives. In countries where the running of society depends upon a sophisticated temporal system using calendrical dates and clock times, time is treated as linear. The past has happened and is no longer accessible, the present is now and is swiftly moving into the past, and the future is yet to come. Time, in this view, has been likened to an arrow, pointing in only one direction (Coveney & Highfield, 1991).[1] People's experience, however, often contradicts this supposed linearity of time, as time appears to slow down, speed up or even stop or reverse (Lockwood, 2005).

Writing in the fourth century BCE, the Greek philosopher Aristotle believed that time was nothing other than the measurement of motion or change, so that if nothing changes time does not pass (Rynasiewicz, 2022). Aristotle's views were pre-eminent for a long time, but centuries later Isaac Newton proposed a different way of viewing time. Writing in the late 17th century Newton argued for what he called absolute time, which passes uniformly whether or not anything in the world changes (Rynasiewicz, 2022). Absolute time cannot be known through direct observation of its passage, but only through mathematical calculations (Rovelli, 2017).

---

[1]Time's arrow is not so straightforward a concept as it might appear. Stephen Hawking (1988), for example, wrote of there being three arrows of time: a psychological arrow, a thermodynamic arrow and a cosmological arrow. All three point in the same direction.

Working in the early years of the 20th century, Albert Einstein synthesised the ideas of Aristotle and Newton, so that 'Time thus becomes part of a complicated geometry woven together with the geometry of space' (Rovelli, 2017, p. 69). The notion of time as the fourth dimension came into being with the concept of space-time, wherein space has three dimensions and time one (Coveney & Highfield, 1991). An event is something which happens at a specific point in space and at a particular time. This refers not only to human events but also to things which happen in the world and wider universe without human intervention, and from the perspective of physics it is more straightforward to think of the event occurring '. . .in a four dimensional space called space-time' (Hawking, 1988, p. 27).

Since Einstein introduced his theory, science has thus supported the idea of the non-linearity of time. Einstein's theory posited that there are multiple times in the universe, all of which are relative to observers and which are dependent upon where observers are and on whether or not they are in motion (Galison, 2003). Time, for example, runs more slowly at low altitudes on earth than at high ones, and this effect is measurable with precision timepieces. Time also runs more slowly for those who are moving at high speeds, for example people travelling by supersonic aircraft (Rovelli, 2017).

Research and thinking about time have continued, building on the work of Einstein. Discoveries made in the field of quantum mechanics have further changed and diminished human ideas and understandings of time, to the extent that it is possible to suggest and to imagine a world in which time does not exist (Rovelli, 2017). Even in such a time-less world, however, things continue to happen, and it is possible to choose variables to measure the change, which do not necessarily have all or any of the hallmarks of what we think of as time (Rovelli, 2017).

One of those variables is movement. The philosophy of movement starts from the point of claiming that the world is made up of processes which may be fairly stable, and which create the phenomena that we observe around us through their repetition. A straightforward example to consider is that of a forest, such as Sherwood Forest, which is a 375 hectare English forest managed by the Royal Society for the Protection of Birds (RSPB). Sherwood Forest is centuries old and it provides a home to a wide range of species of birds and plants, including oak trees in excess of 500 years old and one which is thought to be approximately 1,000 years old. There is stability to be found in the forest, among the older inhabitants, but also constant change through the seasons as, for example, animals mate and breed, and flowers and other plants reproduce, come into flower and then die. Stability of the habitat provides an environment conducive to growth and renewal which could be considered in terms of its temporal elements but could also be analysed by looking at processes of change and movement.[2]

This philosophical approach analyses phenomena from the perspective of motion. Time can also be read as a matter of motion and process, and as incorporating change which is often linked with time Nail (2022). How time is

---

[2]RSPB (2018): Sherwood Forest. https://www.visitsherwood.co.uk/about-sherwood-forest/

related to, or linked with, change is elusive and hard to grasp (Tallis, 2016). Young (2022), as already noted, suggests constant change and movement as perceived by human brains gives us the sense that time is passing. We feel ourselves to be actors in the world, and when we act, we create change and movement, and this makes us feel as if time is passing (Young, 2022).

The idea that time is relative and dependent upon the observer, rather than fixed appears to be compatible with what we know about the world and the wider universe. For example, astronomers use powerful telescopes to look back in time. The James Webb Space Telescope was launched in December 2021 and it has travelled 1.5 million kilometres from the earth in order to look back in time and seek out the first light emitted after the big bang when the universe expanded (Impey, 2021).[3] The telescope is sending pictures back to the earth of far distant galaxies. If time does exist and it is linear, how is it possible, if the past has gone and is lost to the present, to look back into the past in this way? And if time travel into the past is possible, is travel into the future not also possible, outside the pages of science fiction?

Although this has not yet occurred, it has been suggested that physics may eventually eliminate time. This occurrence would have implications for physics but not necessarily for human lives. Time is so deeply embedded in our lives and consciousness that, even if it does not exist, it is unlikely to impact directly on our lives. The probability is that we would be able to continue to live and die as if nothing had changed in respect to time, as we already live and die now without knowing what time is and how it works (Barron et al., 2022).

Baron et al. (2022, p. ix) argue that '...the everyday or 'folk' concept of time...might not exist'. Folk time is '...*what the folk think (almost certainly implicitly) it would take for there to be time in a world*' (Baron et al., 2022, p. 3).[4] They define folk as those people who are not philosophers and suggest that there are potentially multiple folk concepts of time. They make their case by demonstrating that individual agency, which seems to be strongly connected with time, for example through planning for the future, can exist without time. They also utilise some discoveries made about the world which could lead to the conclusion that folk time does not exist and consider recent discoveries in quantum mechanics. Ultimately, they use the notion of causation, separated out from ideas of folk time, to rebuild agency and show that it might be possible to exercise individual agency in the absence of time (Baron et al., 2022, p. 3).

Whether or not time does exist, and whether or not it is an integral element of space-time, it does appear that there are some things we can say about human perceptions and understandings of time. First, there is no universal 'now', and time does not move at the same speed everywhere and always. Second, time does not flow in a linear direction from the past, through the present and into the future

---

[3]European Space Agency, Webb: Seeing farther https://www.esa.int/Science_Exploration/Space_Science/Webb
Goddard Space Flight Center: James Webb Space Telescope https://webb.nasa.gov/index.html
[4]Italics in original text.

(Rovelli, 2017). Third, humans have developed multiple, complex time narratives, which are socially and culturally dependent. They help us to make sense of the changes which we observe, experience and think about. Time is thus an abstract concept and one to which humans have contributed much in its development (Tallis, 2016).

The time narrative which forms the basis of how we understand time in the global north is the one in which time flows, from the past, through the present and into the future. Modernity, with its emphasis on rational thought and scientific thinking, created the conditions for the development and refining of increasingly sophisticated and accurate timepieces and calendrical systems. Together, these have enabled the establishment of complicated social lives, with people meeting, working, learning and travelling efficiently through the use of time tabled and rhythmic patterns possible because of clocks and calendars. Such a way of perceiving time is pervasive in the 21st century, as individuals often feel that time is in short supply and that they never have enough time to complete all the tasks that they feel they should do (Giddens, 1991; Kaufman-Scarborough & Lindquist, 2003).

Perhaps the most plausible notion of time for humans is to be found in the rhythms of our lives and deaths, from the need to sleep, to eat, to drink, to reproduce the species, to die. The human body, like that of all living creatures, is considered by chronobiologists to be a timepiece which interacts with the external environment to keep track of time. This is necessary in order to ensure the survival of the organism and that its physiological needs are met. Speleologist Michel Siffre carried out research in the early 1960s, in which he isolated himself in a cave in the French Alps for two months. He had no access to timepieces nor to the natural shifts of daylight to darkness and back again. When he woke from sleep Siffre would call his team who were waiting at the entrance to the cave, and again when he ate and just before he went to sleep, so that they could track his days (Foer & Siffre, 2008). While his body kept to a rhythm which was more or less that of a day 24 hours long, his sense of calendrical time was out by almost a month. Siffre's work suggested that body clocks, or circadian clocks as they are called, are reasonably accurate in terms of telling the body when it needs rest, or to wake, or to eat and drink, but not at all accurate in assessing calendrical time (Hussey, 2022; Klein, 2007). These findings have been replicated by other studies since then, supporting Siffre's establishment of the existence of the human body clock (Foer & Siffre, 2008; Van Cauter & Turek, 1986).

Beyond the realms of chronobiology and physics, it is perhaps more useful to think of time as socially constructed, something which humans have created in an effort to exert some sense of control over our lives and, more importantly in this context, our deaths. The technologies which we have constructed to measure and record time give us the perception that it is real and exists independently of us. This is enhanced by the fact that these technologies are based on what is perceived to be time in the universe around us, such as the changing seasons, the rotation of planets around the sun, the hours of daylight and darkness which follow a diurnal and seemingly unchanging pattern. These give the impression that timepieces measure something which has real, objective existence, yet physics has demonstrated that clocks run at different speeds in different locations, and calendars are human-made artefacts measuring an artificial time period (Richards, 1998). The perception of time's reality is also reinforced by the way in which language is used in conversation, which is often laden with time-related terms. Bereaved participants, for example, in study 1 stated that they had not thought about the experience of their relative dying in terms of time, yet when they described that experience their talk was full of time-related language. This will be discussed further in Chapter 6.

Is there then a distinction to be made between the notion of natural time, perhaps as evidenced in the body's circadian rhythms and the seasonal changes of the global years, and the notion of social time as experienced by people? Tempting as it may seem to take this approach, it would not be helpful to do so. The people whose deaths form the basis of this book had embodied lives, which are necessarily subject to certain biological and physiological facts of life. They also, however, experience time as social creatures which extends beyond the basic bodily needs. As Adam notes in her text on time and social theory, '...time is still a fact of life but it has emerged as a multi-layered, complex fact of life; multiple in its forms and levels of expressions' (Adam, 1990, p. 169).

Measuring Time

Humans have a long history of attempting to measure and record time through the development of calendars and timepieces and of the refinement and improvement of existing clocks and calendars. Clocks, of whatever kind they are and however accurate they might be, measure the seconds, minutes and hours of their 12 or 24 hour cycle. This pattern is continually repeated, without revealing anything more than time of day or night (Duncan, 1999). Calendars denote time as consisting of just one day which is part of a continuing flow of past, present, future. Once the relevant square on the calendar has passed it cannot be revisited and it gives nothing away about where in time that square on the calendar might be (Duncan, 1999).

The Calendar

It seems as if humans have long had the desire to record and mark down the passage of time. Around 37,000 years ago the paintings which humans left for future generations to see changed from being abstract designs to paintings and drawings of animals. These animals would be of the kinds that the painters were familiar with in their daily lives, and which they hunted for food. Beside the picture of the animal there are often to be found dots and lines. These have been found in cave paintings across Europe, and it has been accepted that the dots and lines represented some form of counting and communication system. A new analysis has taken this further, suggesting that this is, in fact, a form of calendar. In this reading, the dots and lines in sequence '...present ethological information as a seasonal calendar' with important information about the animals' lives conveyed in terms of lunar months (Bacon et al., 2023, p. 6).

The first recognisable and known calendar was established in Egypt in 4236 BCE. The Egyptian calendar had originally been based on the lunar cycle, but awareness that this was not accurate enough to meet their needs prompted the development of a calendar based on the perceived movement of the sun. The new calendar was a civil one, not religious, and it was based in a year of 365 days in length (Duncan, 1999). Since then, many different calendars have been developed and used, and most religions have their own calendar based around their festivals and holy days (Richards, 1998).

It has been difficult for societies to reconcile their calendars with the patterns on which they are notionally based. The time division represented by a month relates to the lunar cycle, and the period of time during which the moon travels around the earth, yet months in calendars in use in the United Kingdom, for example, differ in the number of days. The term 'year' refers to the rotation of the earth around the sun and the seasons, yet neither occur within the exact number of days which we take to represent a year. Both months and years, therefore, are somewhat inconsistent as measures of the length of time passing (Holford-Strevens, 2005; Richards, 1998).

Calendars have been reviewed and revised many times, and efforts made to coordinate them internationally. The Julian calendar of 45 BCE is a familiar basis of many calendars in the 21st century, and it is based in a 12 month, 365.25 day cycle providing for the leap day every fourth year which is intended to bring the years back into synchronicity (Garfield, 2016). The Chinese calendar, however, operates on a 12 year cycle, in which the years are named after animals (Kumaar, 2022). In the 21st century, most countries use the Gregorian calendar, which was invented by Pope Gregory XIII in 1582, as a way of facilitating international relations in a global world (Kumaar, 2022). This makes it easier to coordinate cross-country communications and obviates the need to keep track of the differences, such as the year that is numbered 2023 in the Gregorian calendar is the year of the Rabbit in the Chinese calendar.

Calendars in the 21st century may be printed, and often come with pictures and spaces to write in appointments and reminders. Electronic calendars are also available for use on computers and smartphones and these enable the sharing of appointments and data between system users. Users of such calendars may become used to appointments mysteriously appearing in them, placed by others within their local system.

Timepieces

Measuring time during each individual day is not straightforward, either, as the 24 hour period may begin and end at different points during that 24 hour period, depending upon the social and historical context. For example, for ancient Egyptians the day began at sunrise, in Jewish and Muslim cultures the day starts at sunset and in countries in the global north it begins at midnight as it did for the ancient Romans and does for China (Holford-Strevens, 2005).

Ancient Egypt was a temporally sophisticated culture, and considered that a day consisted of 24 hours, divided into 12 hours of day and 12 hours of night (Holford-Strevens, 2005). Egypt was also home to the earliest surviving water clock, dated to about 1400 BCE. This was a calibrated vessel which used the decreasing level of water to mark the passage of time. It could function effectively during daylight and darkness and formed the basis of time measurement for some

3,000 years (Foulkes, 2019). The water clock, or clepsydra, had an advantage over the sundial, which required sun in order to mark passing time. Eventually, however, the invention of the mechanical clock removed the need for daylight and sunshine or water to measure time.

Pendulum clocks were invented in the 17th century and these were much more accurate than sundials or water clocks (Margolis, 2018). They, in their turn, were superseded in the search for ever greater accuracy. The British government in the 18th century offered a prize for the person who could develop an accurate timepiece which would enable efficient navigation for seagoing craft. The prize was won by John Harrison, who created a clock in which he replaced the pendulum with springs and wheels which could withstand the motion of a ship at sea in a way that the pendulum could not. Through the coordination of London time as shown on the chronometer, and the stars, mariners could chart their location at sea much more accurately. John Harrison continued to work on iterations of his clock after the initial, seagoing trial which had appeared successful, and he was eventually awarded the promised prize, although at a reduced level (Klein, 2007; Sobel, 1995).

Mechanical timepieces have largely been replaced by quartz clocks and watches, the first of which was made in 1927 in the United States. The development of the caesium atomic clock began in 1955, and while these are still produced and in use, a new generation of atomic clocks is in development. Each generation of clocks has been more accurate than the previous one, measuring time to tiny fractions of a second (Margolis, 2018).

Alongside increasing accuracy of the measurement of passing seconds, minutes and hours attempts have also been made to standardise time on a worldwide basis. Time varied between countries but also within countries so that, for example, in England the time of day would differ between London and Bristol. This made it difficult to run an efficient railway service as it was hard to know when a train might arrive given the different time zones through which it passed. In 19th century Great Britain, therefore, the railway companies began to draw up their timetables using Greenwich Mean Time (Holford-Strevens, 2005). Other countries also standardised their time zones, and in 1884, an international conference held in the United States agreed on the prime meridian being that which passed through Greenwich in London. This was the standard until the 1960s, with the globe divided into separate time zones related to the Greenwich meridian (Holford-Strevens, 2005). In 1967, Universal Coordinated Time was accepted globally as the standard, with Greenwich Mean Time being one time zone alongside zones such as Central European or Azores Summer Time.[5]

Personal ownership of domestic timepieces expanded during the second half of the 17th and first half of the 18th centuries in England. Inventories written for the purposes of probate show, for example, that between the 1670s and the 1720s, the number of estates which included clocks increased from nine to 34% in an

---

[5]For more information about Universal Coordinated Time, see 'UTC – The World's Time Standard': https://www.timeanddate.com/time/aboututc.html and time zones, see 'Time Zone Abbreviations': https://www.timeanddate.com/time/zones/

amalgamation of data from eight areas of the country. As a relatively expensive item, it is interesting to note that it was not only the wealthiest households which owned clocks and that ownership was spread between London, towns of different sizes and rural areas (Glennie & Thrift, 2009).

In the 21st century, much of the world's population has access to accurate timekeeping through a computer or smartphone. These offer instant access to accurate data on date and time, such that an individual need never be out of touch with time, providing they have access to the internet or a mobile phone network (Harkin & Kuss, 2021). It is also straightforward to find out the equivalent time in a different global time zone; there may be no universal now, but the connectedness offered by the World Wide Web appears to reduce the separation presented by the existence of different time zones.

Timepieces and calendars are constructs, developed by humans as attempts to measure and to tame time. The week is a good example of the constructed nature of human time; the seven day period is not linked to any natural processes but created by humans and reinforced through use and habit. To say what day of the week it is, is to refer to the past and make the claim that seven days have passed since it was last this day of the week (Henkin, 2021). The existence of clocks and calendars, ostensibly organised in relation to the seasons and the lunar cycle, can give the impression that it is possible to control time (Garfield, 2016; Richards, 1998). It seems as if we know what time is because we can count the seconds and the years, yet human experience simultaneously suggests that there is more to time than its measurement. At different points in our lives we can experience time as if it is misbehaving, going swiftly or slowly, standing still or even seeming to go backwards, while the clock continues to tick and the calendar marks down the days (Adam, 2004).

The endeavour to measure time, and the desire to do so, is a collective effort on the part of societies. Individuals use timepieces and calendars, and their understandings of how time works, but they know about these artefacts because they are part of, and socialised into, a particular social setting. Human perceptions of time are produced and reproduced on a daily basis during interactions and relationships with others, but there is a power imbalance to be observed in the influence that any individual has in the process. This will form part of a later discussion in Chapters 4 and 7.

Differing Human Perceptions of Time

Humans go about their lives, behaving as if time were not a problem. Perhaps unsurprisingly, given that there is no universal now and that the nature and properties of time are uncertain, how time is perceived appears to be largely socially and culturally dependent. Understanding of time, and how it works in any society, is deeply embedded in people's consciousness, learnt as they learn to become members of that society.

In the global north, we know that time flows in a linear direction; we see it as we ourselves and other people visibly age; we see the change from day to night and back again; we see the seasons change, the sun rise and set, even though we know that the sun does no such thing. However, we also know that we do not necessarily experience the passage of time in a straightforward linear fashion, we have flashbacks to the past and dreams of the future; we speak of time flying or dragging (Ogden et al., 2022).

Such a linear way of viewing time is not ubiquitous. There has been much debate about whether such a thing as an African view of time exists and, if it does, what constitutes it. For example, one perspective is that African people do not have an abstract notion of time but, rather, view it as something which is experienced. The corollary of this is that the near future, in terms of such things as the seasons or events that will take place soon, form part of the African understanding of time, but the future as an abstract notion does not (Widlok et al., 2020). Leaving aside debate about the likelihood of the people inhabiting an entire continent taking the same perspective on time, and the probability of differences drawn from local cultural and historical contexts, it does demonstrate that the linear view which is dominant in the global north is not the only way (Adam, 2002).

Language is powerful in offering boundaries for the ways in which we can think and talk about concepts. In some languages, such as Swahili, there are words only for the present and the past and no specific word for the future (Cipriani, 2013). This does not mean, however, that people who speak Swahili are unable to conceive of a future in relation to themselves and that they lack the linguistic ability to convey this conception to others (Widlok et al., 2020).

A linear view is not the only way in which societies have perceived time. The Nuer of southern Sudan, for example, were described by Evans-Pritchard (1939) as having a concept of time which was based in the social rhythm which comes from moving from their village to their camp and back again. This, in turn, was dependent upon whether the season was wet or dry and the consequent availability of water (Evans-Pritchard, 1939). Such a way of thinking about time would fit well with the view of a world in which change and movement are the key concepts, rather than time; the Nuer moved their households in synchronisation with the rhythms of the natural world and lived where water was available (Nail, 2022; Young, 2022).

Another way of perceiving time is as cyclical, with life and death part of an unending circle which has no beginning and no end (Baggini, 2018). Such a view may seem to be common; the seasons repeat in an apparently never ending cycle, bringing new life each spring. Human bodies, like those of all living creatures, have hearts which beat, blood which circulates and lungs which breathe in and out with air, in a cycle which continues in motion until death (Fuchs, 2018). And the cycle continues after death as the body continues to change with the processes of decomposition and the action of insects (Westcott, 2018).

Some cultures and religions take a hybrid view of linear and cyclical time. In Islamic thought, for instance, the occasional appearance of prophets demonstrates the cyclical nature of history, yet simultaneously moves human history forward in a linear fashion (Baggini, 2018). There is therefore no clear cut distinction between linear and cyclical perspectives on time. Some cultures have taken the view that, because an individual lives in a place as well as a time and the two are closely linked, one should not think about the time at which a person lives without also considering the place (Baggini, 2018). This perhaps links with the astronomical view of the four dimensional space-time (Hawking, 1988).

What seems obvious to one social group in terms of what time is and how it works is therefore not necessarily obvious to another group. How we perceive and utilise ideas about time is context dependent, varying across social, geographical and temporal boundaries. It is also the case that the ways in which people experience time and its passage vary, depending upon the circumstances and the kind of experience they are having.

Experiencing Time

Clocks operate as symbols of the time which humans create within their societies, and the more complex the social setting is, the more complex are its temporal arrangements. Time is not the same for everyone, everywhere; in any individual setting there are people who have more, or less, time, just as there are those with more, or less, control over their own lives. Power over the time that an individual has, and the ways in which that time can be used, is linked with class structure and power relations (Nowotny, 1994).

The perception that time is linear with its passage marked by the tick of the clock from the past, through the present and into the future, might suggest that time will be experienced as evenly flowing. This is not, however, necessarily the case. People experience time in different ways in different situations, and they do so without apparent concern, despite the belief that time does, in fact, pass with regularity. Evidence will often reinforce the idea of time's reality and regularity, for example, through the way in which leaves on a tree seem to turn brown overnight during autumn, or the swift developmental changes which babies make as they grow older. That is, even when their learning tells them otherwise, people will experience time as irregular and erratic; as Adam (1995) points out, ordinarily people do not look behind the straightforward ideas of time which underpin life.

Time and its exploration is not only the province of academics, of course. Writers of fiction also engage with the theme of time and some, such as the novelist and playwright J.B. Priestley, have expended much effort and creativity in examining and sharing ideas about time. Priestley was fascinated with the notion of multiple time, in which the past, the present and the future can be simultaneously available to human understanding (Matz, 2012). He wrote a series of seven plays about time, including *Time and the Conways* and *An Inspector Calls*, which explored characters' lives and relationships and how these are influenced by the temporal landscapes in which the dramas take place. For the playwright, theatre acted as a vehicle to bring new ways of experiencing time to the theatre-going public, and he used the medium well to suggest, for example, that the future may influence the present (Matz, 2012). Although first performed during the 1930s and 1940s these plays, in particular *An Inspector Calls*, still appeal to audiences in the 21st century, both in theatres and on the television.

When people do have a reason and the opportunity to explore their views and experiences on time, they respond with wide ranging responses and ideas which are linked to their personal circumstances and beliefs, and these experiences are subject to shifts. Human lives are enveloped by a multitude of times, most of which are implicit and taken for granted, and which Adam describes as 'my' time, 'our' time and 'other' time (1995, p. 12). Any or all of these times may be involved in the experiences which individuals have, and social science research can explore these while adding to our understanding of human experiences of time. There are many studies and modes of experience, but there is space here for only a few which are particularly pertinent to the subject matter of this book.

Time's Suspension

There are occasions in people's lives when it can seem to them as if time is suspended, and as if it no longer passes (Baraitser, 2017). Sometimes, this experience will be related to time spent waiting. Most people will be familiar with the concept of waiting, perhaps for the bus to go to work or school, or for the kettle to boil. Waiting, like time itself, is a concept that is difficult to define, although well understood by those who engage in the process (Schweizer, 2008). The time implications of waiting may pass almost without notice, as part of quotidian life, and with no special significance involved. However, there are occasions when waiting is of great importance in people's lives, such as when waiting for the results of medical tests or exam results in the hope of a positive outcome. Time may also appear to be suspended when an individual waits in the opposite of hope; they wait in dread for an inevitable but undesirable outcome. In a study of prisoners' perspectives on future time, for example, Carvalho et al. (2018) found that it was common for prisoners to perceive time as suspended while they were incarcerated, and to believe that it would begin to pass again once they were released from prison.

Zigon (2018) conducted ethnographic research among people who waited and hoped in post-Soviet Moscow. One group of Muscovites struggled to find anything good to hope for from their futures, believing that there was little they could do to change the likelihood of a negative outcome. However, while one might describe their waiting as passive, in that they felt unable to act in any meaningful way which could influence the outcome for the better, it was also the case that some people expressed the need to maintain hope so that they could live an ethical life (Zigon, 2018). The maintenance, or non-maintenance, of hope can have an effect on the way in which waiting time is experienced. Those who are waiting in relation to something important to them may experience feelings of uncertainty. They may hope for a positive outcome at the end of their period of waiting, but they may also be aware that this is neither certain nor even likely (Janeja & Bandak, 2018). For some in this position, time will be suspended, but for others, it may appear to behave in a more flexible way.

Fluid Time

Bauman (2005, 2006) proposed that we live in what he termed liquid, or fluid, modern times. This has implications for how people can live, as everything is in continual flux and people have no choice but to live with uncertainty. Everything is open ended, so that a decision made today may need to be revisited tomorrow, in the light of changing circumstances. The task that everyone is set by society is to be an individual, and to demonstrate their individuality in the way that they live and present themselves to others. This is, however, a paradoxical thing to attempt. Society forces on people the task of being an individual who must be different to all other individuals. However, the paradox comes when we realise that in fact all individuals are alike and that difference is only understood and accepted through the use of shared tokens, which demonstrate to other people the ways in which we are different. The tokens which signal a person's simultaneous difference and social acceptability are various and may include such things as having the right smartphone, going to the gym, dressing appropriately, living in the right place, taking care of one's health, posting appropriately on social media and so on (Bauman, 2005). Such tokens do not include flouting social hygiene rules nor dying in a socially inappropriate way (Caswell, 2021). Living in fluid modern times carries with it implications, too, for how people experience and manage their time.

Katz and Greene (2021) report on how the families of people who are missing in Israel deal with and experience time in relation to their loss. The families of missing people live with uncertainty on a daily basis, and managing time is one way of imposing order on events and how they feel about those events. Members of the families who are left behind by the missing person do this in different ways, through the establishment of a temporal regime which suits them. In their analysis, Katz and Greene (2021) have developed three temporal regimes which family members utilise.

The first of these is parallel time, whereby family members think about their missing person living on a different timeline which runs parallel with the family's own. There is a resonance here with Adam's concept of 'my' and 'our' times (Adam, 1995, p. 12). The second temporal regime posited by Katz and Greene (2021) is that of presumed dead time. This brings about a resolution to parallel time and all the difficulties and uncertainties that it represents may come to an end through the decision to presume that the missing person is dead. It may be considered that this could reunite parallel times with linear times, except that presumed death brings no confirmation of the death of the missing person. The third temporal regime proposed by the authors is perpetual time. In this regime, the disappearance and the experience of it may be described by families in the past tense, as if it happened during a period which is now over, although there is no presumption of the death of the missing person. In this way of thinking about time, the missing person '...no longer carries the status of alive, but is also not presumed dead' (Katz & Greene, 2021, p. 69).

The high level of uncertainty which the families of missing people endure, sometimes over a long period of time, puts at risk assumptions that we might usually hold about linear time and its ubiquity. The work of Katz and Greene (2021) demonstrates how in the context of a society which is in a state of constant flux (Bauman, 2005) '...families of the missing relationally construct and move among different temporal regimes...' (Katz & Greene, 2021, p. 72). Time itself is not fixed and neither is the way in which people experience it.

Liminal Time

To be in a liminal status is to be in a position of ambiguity. Van Gennep (1909) developed the concept as part of his work on rites of passage, which occur when an individual is in the process of undergoing a significant change to their social status from, for example, child to adult or single person to married person. There are three stages to the rites of passage which can both assist an individual through significant life changes and also mark those changes (Davies, 2002). The pre-liminal phase is separation, during which individuals are separated from their old status, such as when a child reaches puberty and ceases to be a child. The next or liminal phase is that of transition, which will involve the no-longer child, now an adolescent, making the move from the world of children to that of adults. The final, or post-liminal phase is that of incorporation, during which the adolescent becomes incorporated into the world of the adults and takes on the rights and responsibilities of adulthood (Van Gennep, 1909).

Turner (1969) further developed the work of Van Gennep (1909) and rites of passage, extending the range of possible ways in which the concept of liminality could be used, writing that 'Liminal entities are...betwixt and between...' (Turner, 1969, p. 95). Turner has been accused of using the term liminal to refer to any short period of time between two stages when there is a shift in power relations (Wels et al., 2011). However, despite critiques of Turner's flexibility in his usage of the term liminal, many scholars now use the term in a way which is in keeping with the betwixt and between notion, but not necessarily with van Gennep's stricter usage of it as a phase during a rite of passage (Turner, 1969; van Gennep, 1909).

One example may be found in Dorow and Jean's (2022) study of liminal time in the lives and experiences of what they describe as 'fly-in fly-out workers' (p. 681). These are employees who work in industries such as oil, and who spend some time at home and some of their time living and working away from home. The workers develop temporal tactics which enable them to manage their liminal time and status, which Dorow and Jean describe through the use of four themes. First, some workers engage in 'routinising' whereby they stick to routines both in their work time and during their down time while away from home. For some workers, this is straightforward as they are suited by their characters to engage with routine, but for others, it was much more difficult to achieve the maintenance of routines (Dorow & Jean, 2022, p. 694).

The second tactic described was that of 'disrupting', with workers making efforts to disrupt the routines and rhythms of the workspace (Dorow & Jean, 2022, p. 695). A third tactic used was that of 'syncing with "outside" time'. The attempt to synchronise with external times was particularly important for workers who wished to stay in touch with people at home through phone or video calls (Dorow & Jean, 2022, p. 696). The final tactic described was that of 'orienting to the future', by which employees orientated themselves towards goals for the future as a way of increasing their ability to remain in the present (Dorow & Jean, 2022, p. 697).

Dorow and Jean (2022) take a flexible approach to the use of the concept liminality (Wels et al., 2011). The workers who participated in their research would normally spend one or two weeks on the oil rig at a time and they are not necessarily experiencing a major life change during their time offshore. However, their paper shows the importance of time, and how that is experienced, in relation to individuals who are in a liminal status. They also demonstrate the sophistication with which individuals can approach their understanding of time (Dorow & Jean, 2022).

Timescapes

Human lives and experiences are saturated with time, and there is nothing we do which does not have temporal implications. It is logical, therefore, to consider time as a key facet of the endeavour to understand human activity and relations. We have also seen how complex the human relationship with time is, and it is apparent that it is not sufficient to ask questions about the when of linear time. Adam's notion of the timescape is useful here. She describes a timescape as a cluster of temporal features, suggesting a range of temporal features that a timescape might comprise, such as time frames, temporality, tempo, timing, time point and so on (Adam, 2004, p. 144). She uses the term timescape because it '...indicates, first, that time is inseparable from space and matter, and second, that context matters' (Adam, 2004, p. 143).

Degen (2018) explored the regeneration of one of the Ramblas in Barcelona from the perspective not just of space but also of temporalities. She described this as a kind of time-space. The research was a longitudinal study of the remaking of the physical space, as well as of the interdependent and divergent temporalities that are involved in the remaking and experiencing of this time-space. The temporalities of different social groups involved in the regeneration project, from the urban planners through to the users of the space, all had their own sense and modalities of time.

The research showed that '...different social groups have distinctive temporal relations to places that shape their experiences, uses and perceptions...' (Degen, 2018, p. 1089). By working with the differing temporalities of the groups involved in the regeneration, Degen has demonstrated both the importance of time in relation to the development of public space and also how the various features of the timescape are key to this understanding (Adam, 2004; Degen, 2018).

Hidden Temporal Rhythms

Zerubavel (1981) describes the regular temporal patterns which exist in social life, but which are largely unnoticed and disregarded because we are so familiar with them and take them for granted. He argues that there are four major temporal dimensions to be found in any specific happening or situation. The first dimension is that of sequential structure, which tells us the order in which things will occur. The second dimension, that of duration, informs us how long something may last, while the third, temporal location, reveals when the event will happen. The fourth and final parameter is the rate of recurrence, and this shows how often the event or situation will take place (Zerubavel, 1981, p. 1).

Our familiarity with the temporal patterning of life means that it is most likely to become obvious when that pattern is broken. For example, when a household phone rings in the middle of the night it may cause those living in the house to feel surprised or uneasy, not because of the phone ringing per se, but because of the 'unusual temporal location' of its ringing (Zerubavel, 1981, p. 24).

Zerubavel proposed that time is one of the dimensions of the public and private, writing that '*...time functions as one of the major dimensions of social organization along which involvement, commitment and accessibility are defined and regulated in modern society*' (Zerubavel, 1981, p. 141).[6] The separation between the public and private spheres of social life is neither distinct nor straightforward, and the same caveat applies to the separation of private and public time (Brewer, 2018; Zerubavel, 1981). Night-time is generally regarded as private, a time when people may expect to have privacy to sleep in a safe and secure environment. However, there are exceptions to this. Some people work at night and so are necessarily to be found within the public sphere, both temporally and geographically. There are also circumstances when night-time privacy may be broken for legitimate reasons, such as in case of illness or another emergency (Zerubavel, 1981).

The temporal rhythms and patterns as described by Zerubavel are important. They demonstrate how much we take for granted in relation to the impact of time on our lives. They underpin our sense of time and what the nature of time is on a day by day basis. When something happens which disrupts the regular temporal pattern of our lives we are forced to reconsider our view of time.

There have been many studies conducted of time use which explore the patterns, and the deviations from patterns, in the way in which individuals use their time. Craig and Mullan (2011), for example, analysed time use data from Australia, Denmark, France and Italy relating to the way in which mothers and fathers share childcare. Vagni (2022) also analysed time use data in order to explore family life in the United Kingdom, specifically how time together with partners and children impacted on well-being. Study findings demonstrated that fathers enjoyed family time more than mothers did, which the author suggested was the result of the unequal division of labour during family time between parents (Vagni, 2022).

---

[6]Italics in original text.

The Social Nature of Temporal Experience

The ways in which people experience time discussed in the previous section are not exhaustive, and many more perspectives and conceptualisations could be drawn upon. What the selected approaches have in common is that they are social, and people are able to make use of them by drawing on shared understandings to which they have access through complex processes of socialisation into a society's norms and practices. Time is a taken for granted part of every human activity and, whether or not it has an independent existence outside human observation, the ways in which time is experienced, utilised and understood by people is a social construction (Bluedorn, 2002). Our understandings of time are, and have been, created in collaboration with other people over a long period of time. We benefit from the insights and knowledge of our ancestors. How time is perceived and experienced depends, as has already been noted, on social and historical context (Bluedorn, 2002).

Time as Social Construct

There are many facets of human life which appear to be obviously occurring phenomena and things. Some, such as the need to eat and drink and for the species to reproduce, are requirements that derive from the fact that humans are animals and from the need for individuals and the species to survive. Others, such as the use of tools, the writing and reading of books and ideas about time and its uses, may not impinge on the survival of the species. However, one thing which all kinds of activities have in common is that the way in which they are carried out depends upon how people interpret and define them. When a person dies, for example, there is a dead body which those who survive can either ignore and leave where the person died or they can move and manage the body. Corpses decay and may have the potential to infect living people with diseases, so it makes sense for society to ensure the disposal of the body in a way that will prevent this occurring. How this disposition of human corpses happens is an example of social construction in action. Throwing the body off a cliff or down a gorge, casting it into the sea, onto a bonfire, into a waste bin or burying it in a hole in the ground are all possibilities. However, all societies have social rituals around how the dead body of a deceased person should be managed, because we value our dead as people who are now deceased. The ways in which societies and individuals handle their dead are not part of the natural world, they are socially constructed and dependent upon social and historical context. Time is also a social construct in the ways that people understand, utilise, measure and record it. Despite efforts to ground time in the natural world individuals rarely use reference points such as sunrise or sunset to time their activities. Instead, constructs such as calendars and clocks are used to coordinate activities and record times (Berger & Luckmann, 1967; Luckmann, 1991; Sachs, 2001; van Schaik & Wojtkowiak, 2022).

Conclusion

This book makes no attempt to come to any conclusion as to whether time exists and, if it does, what it might be. It addresses the topic of time of death from the perspective of human understandings, experiences and utilisation of time. We do know that time from the human point of view is a social construct which has been produced and reproduced over time and place. As members of a social setting, we each know and understand how to work with the temporal regimes which operate in that setting. We use time as a way of measuring and recording changes which occur and as a means of organising experiences and relating them to each other. This helps to make sense of our lives as we live through time, grow up and grow older and can observe this through the interrelatedness of our experiences.

Shared ways of measuring the passage of time permit members of a society to synchronise activities and organise the collective aspects of life (Zerubavel, 1981). Shared understandings enable people to share and make sense of their own, and others', experiences of time. Individuals are able to deal with the apparent contradiction involved in knowing that time is linear and immutable yet is still sometimes experienced as if it was otherwise. It is well known, for example, that time passes swiftly when an individual's attention is engaged or when they are in a novel situation with a vast array of new information to process, and that the reverse is also the case (Danckert & Allman, 2005; Yates, 2019). Such knowledge is long standing. Iago says, at the end of Act II of the play *Othello*, 'Pleasure and action make the hours seem short' at the point when his plans are falling into place (Shakespeare, 1604). Time is also said to pass more quickly for people as they age; this is also not a new phenomenon, although the cause is unclear and may be related to cognitive function and levels of sadness or happiness (Droit-Volet, 2019; Hancock & Hancock, 2014).

The use of calendars demonstrates a shared concept of time and the months, weeks and days as a measure of a year's worth of the passing of time. When calendars are used to record events and appointments they can also be a form of communication. For example, it is suggested that cave paintings conveyed temporal information, in a fashion similar to the use of electronic invitations to online meetings within the cyber world (Bacon et al., 2023). It appears that concepts of time have been a feature of human life since the early years of humanity's existence, and that attempts to communicate and synchronise time have also been part of ongoing human activity.

The next chapter will move the discussion on to the topic of death, considering what death is and the context within which it occurs in the 21st century.

Chapter 3

Considering Death

Introduction

In order to answer the question, 'when is the time of death?' it is necessary to have some understanding of what death is, as well as what time is. Death, like time, is a concept which appears to be straightforward until we try to define it, and then we realise that it is another mystery. There are myriad questions to be asked about death and its nature. For example, is death simply the end of existence of the physical body of an individual human, and if it is, does that refer to the moment when they stop breathing, when their heart stops beating or to some other physiological event? There are also questions about what else, if anything, might be involved in the death of a person. For individuals who hold a religious faith, it may be that they believe there is a soul or spirit which outlasts the physical body and which has an ongoing life in some form. This offers the possibility of people who knew each other in life being reunited in an afterlife or even of the living communicating with the deceased person (Park, 2021).

Living in an increasingly secular society makes this appear to be less of an option for a growing number of people, although data from the British Social Attitudes survey of 2018 suggest that belief in a deity is not a necessary requirement for belief in an afterlife (Voas & Bruce, 2019).[1] Does this therefore necessarily mean that individuals must accept that once a person they care about has undergone biological death, that is the end of their existence? What happens to a person and the relationships they had with others once their body has died and begun to decompose? This chapter is concerned with exploring the nature of death and some of our understandings of it, as part of the process of exploring the concept 'time of death'.

Humans have created sophisticated narratives to make sense of time, in the face of the impossibility of knowing what it is or even whether or not it has objective

---

[1]British Social Attitudes surveys are run annually by the National Centre for Social Research: https://www.bsa.natcen.ac.uk/latest-report/british-social-attitudes-36/religion.aspx In the 36th such survey, run in 2018, 39% of respondents stated a belief in god, whereas 42% stated that they believed in an afterlife.

Time of Death, 29–46
Copyright © 2024 Glenys Caswell
Published under exclusive licence by Emerald Publishing Limited
doi:10.1108/978-1-80455-005-220241003

existence. These narratives are socially and culturally dependent, and they make time appear to be an objective thing which can be measured and recorded. Although this may not be the case, it does mean that individuals can take time for granted, going about their lives without needing to debate time and its reality on a daily basis. One of the downsides, however, to accepting the existence and relentless passage of time is that it brings with it knowledge of the fact that at some time, all people, including ourselves, will die. Human lives are finite and time brings everything, including lives, to an end.

For those who accept the linearity of time perspective, as is common in the global north, the perception of life and death as the individual is born, lives and dies follows the same kind of thinking; we believe that we have lived through the past, are living in the present and will live in the future. Our future ends when we die, but we can relive the past through our memories, and those memories can help us in our attempts to shape our futures. However, if we were to think of time as cyclical, we might see ourselves as part of a cycle of birth and then death, after which the decomposing body returns to the earth and nourishes new life forms. We would see our relationship with time and with other aspects of life and death, differently, for our bodies will decompose after death and eventually become part of the earth.

This book takes the view that human life is a reality, and that we are more than digital creations taking part in a computer simulation, as has been suggested as a possibility (Francis, 2014). This chapter takes as its focus death which, if life is real, is also real. It argues that death is a process rather than an event, and that processes of change are integral to dying and death. It begins with a consideration of the human awareness of the fact of mortality and the efforts that people may make to avoid the full impact of this knowledge. Next, the question as to what death is will be asked and an answer attempted by looking first at social death, then at the death of the body and the impact which technology has on death. Some of the forms which death takes will then be considered, both in the sense of the most common kinds of dying and those which are unusual in the 21st century. This is followed by a brief consideration of emotional responses to death, and this chapter concludes by outlining what will be taken forward about death for the discussion about time of death.

Mortality Awareness

At the end of his play *Sheppey*, Somerset Maugham retold the ancient Meso-potamian tale of a servant who had encountered death in the marketplace in Baghdad. The servant was terrified and borrowed a horse from his master to flee away from Baghdad and the personification of death. The master himself later encountered death and queried why she had so frightened his servant. Death replied that she had not intended to frighten the man, but on the contrary, she said that she had been surprised to meet the servant in Baghdad, when they had an appointment later that day in Samarra (Maugham, 1933/2017). The implication of the tale, of course, is that the servant fled to Samarra, where he later encountered death again and died. The moral is clear that we cannot cheat death, and it is pointless to try to do so.

In whatever ways members of a society conceive time, they know that they are mortal, and that one day they will die. They may be distracted by the concerns of daily life, but ultimately, they know that they are being-towards-death and know that while they may hope to live for a very long time, the point at which they will die is uncertain, and it could be today (Heidegger, 1962; May 2009). In an effort to stave off the effects of fear which such knowledge potentially generates, people may make attempts to secure their immortality in various ways. They may, for example, hold a religious belief that tells them their soul will endure or they may create a legacy for the future which means that they will be remembered after their death (Cave, 2013). Other individuals may make an attempt to delay their dying for as long as possible, by, for example, following the most up-to-date advice on healthy living and seeking medical help at the first sign of any illness. However, as Bauman (1992) suggests, what this means is that the individual is effectively choosing what they will die from, for it is impossible to make, and enact the choice never to die.

For a small number of people, though, cryonics appears to offer a way to try and evade the finality of death. The idea of cryogenic preservation is to freeze either the whole body or the head immediately after death so that it will be preserved and brought back to life at some point in the future through the use of advanced medical technologies. The expectation is that when the body is revived, whatever caused it to die the first time will be curable so that the person may live again. There are several companies worldwide which offer cryogenic preservation, which is marketed as a second chance at life and as offering the possibility of immortality.[2] The idea was first mooted in the early 1960s, and since then, over 200 people have been cryopreserved, with hundreds more signed up ready for when they die (Dein, 2022).

Menzies and Menzies (2021) have suggested that the evolution of the human brain to its relatively large size compared to those of other living creatures has put us in a position where children as young as five years old become aware of the fact of death. This has the potential to cause death anxiety which can last a lifetime, although studies do suggest that death anxiety may reduce as people grow older. The consequence of this death anxiety is the need to put off or ignore the inevitability of death by seeking some form of 'symbolic or virtual immortality', if the individual is not able to manage the anxiety by religious means (Menzies & Menzies, 2021, p. 20). Human cultures offer many resources for individuals to put together their own strategy for avoidance of the fear of death so much so that societies have sometimes been described as groups of people banded together against death (Berger, 1969).

There are times and places where the discussion of death has been described as a taboo topic. This depends, of course, on what is meant by taboo, which changes across time and space. The claim that death is a taboo topic, that it is something

---

[2]See, for example, The Cryonics Institute, 2022: https://cryonics.org/ or the Alcor Life Extension Foundation, 2020: https://www.alcor.org/

which cannot and must not be spoken of in a social setting, is too strong a claim to apply broadly in the 21st century. Some people may be reluctant to speak about death in some of its aspects, but there is a wide range of literature available on the topic, and it features regularly in the media, whether as part of news stories or fictional representations. Perhaps, for some people, some of the time death is a taboo topic but not for everyone all of the time (Sayer, 2010; Walter, 1991).

It is also the case that the apparent negativity around death and dying, exemplified by claims of death as a taboo topic and thanatophobia or an extreme fear of death and dying does not prevent some people taking an alternative approach towards the knowledge that they must die. The death positivity movement, death cafés, death doulas, soul midwives, talking about dying and the happy death movement are just some of the organisations, events and roles which exist in the 21st century and promote discussion and learning about death and dying (Baldwin, 2017; Koksvik, 2020; Lofland, 1978).

In addition to the consciousness that we have of the fact that we must die, we also have access to collective narratives of time, as well as stories of creation and religion, and myriad other narratives which help in the attempt to assign meaning to human lives. Sometimes, this requires a belief in an existence beyond the life of the physical body, which may take the form of a religiously inspired afterlife. However, it may also be that when a person dies and they no longer have an embodied presence in the world, they will be mourned and remembered by living people, who may cause the deceased's body to be treated in ways which alter the natural processes of change that dead bodies undergo. They may have the body embalmed to delay processes of decay, they may cremate it and change its formulation and they may bury it in a lined coffin which will hold back decomposition. Doing this is about fulfilment of the social responsibility which bereaved people have for the ritual processes concerned with grief and mourning, as well as treating the deceased person with socially appropriate respect (Rugg & Jones, 2019).

As time passes, those who are bereaved will remember the person who died, and they may have many ways of keeping the deceased person socially alive to them. There are time implications here, but that experience of time is different from time as it affects the person who dies. When an individual dies, awareness of time and its effects ceases for them, but their body continues to be subject to the effects of time, as their body will continue to change until it is completely decomposed and broken down (Westcott, 2018). There is a distinction, therefore, to be made between social death and biological death in temporal terms, and this will be discussed further in subsequent chapters.

Humans have illusions of control over death just as they have illusions of being able to control time with clocks and calendars. Healthy living and the skills and resources of medical professionals help to give individuals the illusion that they have some control over their own death, and that they can avoid or evade it if only they try hard enough (Bauman, 1992). However, all must die, and humans do not have any real control over their deaths because whatever they do to try and defer, delay or prevent it, death will still happen. Death will catch us however quickly we ride to Samarra. But what is this death which we are doing our best to sidestep?

What Is Death?

Defining death is not a straightforward task, yet in order to think about the concept time of death, it will be necessary to attempt a definition of what it is that we wish to identify the time of. The word death can refer to a number of different things, including the state of being dead, to part of the process of dying or to the final part of the process which happens when an individual is dying (Luper, 2009; Tomasini, 2017). In everyday language use, it is assumed that the death of a person is the death of their physical body and not their social death which may occur prior to, at the same time as, or after their bodily or biological death (Caswell & O'Connor, 2015). Here, the discussion engages with both social and biological death and the links between them. It asks what each kind of death is, and what effect that technologies may have on their occurrence and timing. It also considers the impact that digital technologies, and the enduring online life that individuals have the potential to leave after their deaths, may have on perceptions about social death (Kasket, 2019).

Social Death

All living creatures undergo biological death, and this includes humans. In so far as we know, however, it is only human beings who also die a social death which relates to the end of their social existence and which does not necessarily coincide with the end of their biological life. Social death, whereby the individual is treated as if dead while still biologically alive, is a concept which is utilised in different contexts and with subtly different meanings. It can refer to individuals who make a decision to disengage with the wider world and enter a period of social death, and it can also apply to individuals who are pushed into the status by others. It has been applied to people who have dementia, to people who are slaves or who have undergone a serious brain injury. The term social death is thus applied to individuals who, for some reason, may be deemed to be no longer fully active human agents (Borgstrom, 2017; Caswell, 2022; Kralova, 2015).

In his study of dying in hospital and the decisions made by clinical staff about whether or not to attempt resuscitation when a patient experienced a cardiac arrest, Sudnow (1967) developed the concept of social death. Clinicians made decisions about resuscitation which were often based on judgements about a patient's moral worth, with the result that some people were treated as if already dead, despite the fact that biologically they were still alive. The consequence of this was that should a patient so classified undergo a cardiac arrest, there would be no attempt at resuscitation (Sudnow, 1967).

It is also the case that many people who are considered to have died continue to have a social existence and relevance even after their funeral has taken place and their body has been buried or cremated. People who knew them continue to think and talk about them, accommodating the deceased person into their ongoing lives. The level at which this occurs is likely to reduce over time, although some who have been bereaved will continue to accord their deceased person social relevance over an extended period of time, perhaps even until they die themselves. In these situations, a measure of agency may be conferred on the deceased by the living, who perhaps make choices by referring to what they believed would have been the deceased person's wishes or who take the deceased individual into account when making their own future decisions (Caswell, 2022, pp. 203–204).

This idea of agency conferred on the deceased individual by living people who knew them when they were alive is different to the agency which may be demonstrated through plans made by a living person prior to their own death for after they have died. A living individual may plan their funeral and do so for many reasons, which can include the desire to control how they are memorialised and presented in the funeral context.[3] This represents a desire to exert agency after biological death, as is the case when an individual disperses their goods after death by virtue of writing a will before death.

The notion of agency being conferred on a person who has died is similar to the idea that human rights may sometimes be conferred on a deceased person. As is the case with the conferring of human rights, the level of agency accorded is limited, and there is no expectation that the individual will be able to exercise their agency independently. Such agency that a person has after undergoing biological death is that which is accorded to them by one or more of the people who knew them when they were alive (Caswell, 2022; Caswell & Turner, 2020; Moon, 2016).

Since the 1990s, there has been a shift in the way in which bereavement and grief are theorised. It is now recognised that people who have been bereaved will often maintain an ongoing relationship with the person who died, sometimes nurturing this bond and finding ways to incorporate them into their ongoing life. In this model, grieving is not about getting over the death and moving on from it but about maintaining continuing bonds with the deceased person (Klass & Steffen, 2018). There is, perhaps, an, as yet, under-explored link between the conscious maintenance of continuing bonds and the conferment of a limited agency on the deceased. However, for the purposes of this discussion, it is sufficient to note that for some individuals, their social death takes place at a later time than their biological death.

Not everyone who dies has family and friends to remember them and accord them ongoing social existence after their death. In this situation, it may be that the post-death processes put in place by the state to deal with death give the deceased individual a temporary revival of social existence, although it is doubtful that individuals in this situation will be accorded social agency (Caswell, 2022; Caswell & O'Connor, 2015). This possibility will be discussed further in Chapter 5.

---

[3]For an example of a funeral planned by the deceased prior to death, see: BBC 11th January 2023, Flash-mob dance at Bristol funeral breaks tradition, https://www.bbc.co.uk/news/av/uk-england-bristol-64223053

Online Social Existence After Biological Death

The online world offers new and rapidly changing ways of attaining a social existence and measure of agency after the death of the biological body. Digital artefacts in many different forms such as social media posts, blogs, website contributions and so on, which have been left by the person when alive, will continue to be available online. Other internet users have the opportunity to interact with them, unless the original creator makes provision for the disposal of their digital data once they have died (Savin-Baden, 2019). Indeed, other internet users may not realise that the person with whom they are interacting is no longer alive.

Before a person dies, it is possible for them to set up the sending of posthumous digital messages to their family and friends (Bassett, 2018). This means that, while alive, an individual can take steps to try and continue their social agency after death, in the hope of continuing to have an impact on others and to do so through the medium of the online world. Continued social existence may also be the unintended consequence of a person not taking steps to manage their online data and what happens to it after their deaths. This may come about because they do not realise the extensiveness of their online footprint or because they do not get round to making a decision and taking action, but the effect is likely to be the same. People may continue to interact with them online as if they were alive. The web may also be used by the living to confer a measure of agency on the deceased, for example by posting messages to them on social media such as Facebook or Twitter, sending them birthday greetings or offering snippets of news from their own lives (Bell et al., 2015; Kasket, 2012, 2019).

Ongoing Social Existence or Social Death

Accepting that the living maintain ongoing bonds with their dead and that such relationships endure acknowledges that the way is open for new methods of relating to those who have died. Digital, as well as physical, artefacts can be utilised in the maintenance of these bonds and are likely to outlast the memories of individuals. The existence of artefacts of whatever kind neither ensures nor guarantees that a person who has died will continue to have a social existence and to exert social agency, but they do offer ways of supporting the possibility (Kasket, 2019; Valentine, 2013).

The markers of social death are less well defined than those of biological death. Often it depends upon the perceptions of others in more powerful social groups, as when an individual is pushed into the status by others because of some characteristic which they have. The time at which an individual enters a period of social death is thus hard to define. To experience social death means that an individual lacks social agency and no longer features as an active social agent in the lives of other people (Mulkay & Ernst, 1991). The very nature of social death thus requires that the individual is unnoticed and not taken into account by others. When someone is unnoticed to an extreme extent, their absence from social groupings is unobserved and their death, whether biological or social, is also unwitnessed and unnoticed.

Despite the difficulty in observing when such a death has occurred, however, the concept of social death is important to the consideration of time of death. It is generally straightforward for a qualified medical professional to know that a person has died biologically, although it may be less straightforward in some instances to tell how long has passed since the death occurred. Sometimes, society's rules will require that the time of death be estimated as closely as possible, but this is not always the case. The prior social death of the individual who has subsequently died biologically is one possible reason for not trying to discover an accurate time of death. This will form the basis for a discussion in Chapter 5. Difficulties involved in assessing when a social death has occurred much later than the biological death, when the individual had a form of ongoing social existence after the death of their body, will be discussed in Chapter 6.

Death of the Body

There is no one definition of biological death or dying which applies in all cultures at all times, and it is also the case that the causes of death have changed over time. In the mediaeval period in northern Europe, for example, people were most likely to die from an infectious disease, by starvation as the result of failed harvests or even from violence, and they could do so at any age; children died frequently (Doig, 2022). Over time, this has changed. In 2019, 55 million people died worldwide and 74% of these deaths were from non-infectious diseases, with heart diseases and cancers the cause of just over half of all deaths (Roser, 2021). Between 1990 and 2019, the age at which people died also changed. In 1990, a quarter of all deaths globally were of children under the age of five, and by 2019, this had reduced to nine per cent. Over the same period of time, the number of deaths of people aged over 70 had increased from a third to a half (Ritchie et al., 2019).

The word 'death' suggests an ending to a life, yet it can also refer to the process which ends with the death of an organism, to the status of being dead or to the final, irreversible moment at which a person may be considered to have died (Tomasini, 2017). The question as to whether death is something which takes place in a moment or whether it is a process taking place over time is one which endures. Azevedo and Othero (2020) suggest that the death of a human happens in a three-phase process. The first phase they describe as dying, which is when the physiological responses to the closing down of the body's organs are underway. The second phase is decease, when cardiac arrest or respiratory failure indicates that the body's vital functions are shutting down, and the final stage is decay when the irreversible process of cellular death is underway and will eventually cover the whole body (Azevedo & Othero, 2020).

For a social scientist such as myself, the medical literature about dying can sometimes be technical and confusing, so I spoke to Dr Stuart Hamilton. Dr Hamilton has been a Home Office Registered Forensic Pathologist in the United

Kingdom since 2008. As part of this role, Dr Hamilton carries out autopsies in criminal and suspicious death cases, as well as in more routine cases for the coroner. He is well versed in the debates about what death is and when it can be said to have occurred. He is also eloquent and generous in sharing his knowledge and understanding.

Dr Hamilton considers that there are three different ways to consider the question of what death is. First, there is the basic human comprehension that we all have that someone is dead when we see their corpse. He said:

> I think most people who have come across a dead person, and certainly my experience many years ago on the wards, is when you come across somebody who is deceased, you know because they are.

It is unclear what it is that makes it seem obvious that the person is dead, but Dr Hamilton thinks it may be the relaxation of the facial muscles which we do not see in a living person.

The second way of defining death which Dr Hamilton describes is the legal concept of death which, in his role as pathologist, he deals with on a daily basis. In the United Kingdom, what happens when an individual dies is governed by legislation, one piece of which states that every death should be certified by a legally qualified medical practitioner. From a legal perspective, the death has not taken place until it has been medically certified, and the implications of this will be discussed further in Chapter 5.

The third way of defining death which Dr Hamilton identified was biological and physiological death. When a body's major organs cease to function and it might be considered that the person has died, there will still be energy in the body's cells. This process takes time, and it is this residual cellular energy which means that organs can be transplanted from one person to another, and that the transplanted organ may still work in the recipient's body. So a person may be biologically dead, but their liver or kidneys retain sufficient energy to continue working in another body; their physiological death occurs later.

Dr Hamilton is a thoughtful man who has reflected much on the nature of his work and what he has learned about the nature of death from it. Overall, it is his belief that:

> I think most of us again who think about these things, as you can imagine we think about it a lot, would say that the best definition of death is the point where the body can no longer support itself. So it's the point where your system simply shuts down. And I think maybe to get a little philosophical I think it's the point where the person you are is gone. So there may be still a bit of electrical activity in your heart, there may be still a little bit of energy left in your kidneys, the sort of thing that allows them to be transplanted, but whatever essentially made you you, has gone and it's not coming back.

The notion of death being about the cessation of whatever it is that makes a person the unique individual that they were is resonant with the 21st century project of the individual. According to this project, each person needs to be noticed and accounted for, and each is expected to make their own choices, decide on the kind of person that they wish to be and then take steps to become that person. Individuals do experience constraints which limit the options available to them, and such constraints may come about through inequitable social positioning which adversely impacts an individual's access to education, employment, housing, financial resources and many other social and cultural goods. Whatever a person's social positioning, however, the pressure is on for individuals to decide what kind of person they want to be and then demonstrate their uniqueness to the rest of the world (Bauman, 2005; Giddens, 1991). Social rhetoric suggests that the existence of the living individual is paramount, and their dying must be accounted for.

On a quotidian level, therefore, a definition of death is needed that can be used to identify when a person has died. This is important, as it opens the way for the accomplishment of the many social obligations that follow on from the occurrence of a death. There is, for instance, the need for the disposal of a body which has become a matter of waste. The body must now be safely removed from the space occupied by the living who may be contaminated by it, however unlikely and unrealistic this is. The diagnosis of death is also needed by the family and friends of the deceased person so that they can engage in the ritual practices required in their social setting in order to deal with the body and processes of mourning. In addition, there are also a range of legal processes which must be carried out (Bradbury, 1999; van Schaik & Wojtkowiak, 2022).

In the 21st century, the medical profession takes the lead in defining what counts as death and in deciding whether and when an individual has died, while the legal system confers legitimacy on this process through procedures of certification and registration of death (AbouZahr et al., 2015; Bishop, 2011). The World Health Organization (WHO) recommends the use of the *International Form of Medical Certificate of Cause of Death* which forms the basis of all statistical data related to death and its causes.[4] Alongside information about the primary and secondary causes of death, the certificate also includes details about the individual, including their name, sex, date of birth and date of death (University of Melbourne, 2016).

How biological death is defined and understood has changed over time. Ancient Greeks believed that life began with the first beat of the heart and ended with the last, and for people of the Jewish and Christian faiths, the taking of the last breath was the indicator of death (Roux-Kemp, 2008). Brain death has increasingly become one of the criteria for determining death, although for some cultures this is problematic. In Japan, for example, there is an expectation that the

---

[4]World Health Organization, 2023, Medical Certification - International form of medical certificate of cause of death. https://www.who.int/standards/classifications/classification-of-diseases/cause-of-death

family of the dying person must consent to the person being considered brain dead, which perhaps comes from the supporting role that is accorded to the family of the dying person (Roux-Kemp, 2008; Terunuma & Mathis, 2021).

The Academy of Medical Royal Colleges (AMRC) in the United Kingdom defines death as: '...the irreversible loss of the capacity for consciousness, combined with irreversible loss of the capacity to breathe' and identifies a number of criteria which can be used to comply with the definition (Academy of Medical Royal Colleges, 2008, pp. 11–20). From a philosophical perspective, it has been suggested that it may be necessary to wait for putrefaction of the body to begin in order to be certain that death has occurred, although less time-consuming methods are used in usual medical practice in the 21st century (Carrasco & Valera, 2021). Historically, various methods to check for death have been used, from holding a mirror to the person's nose to see if they are still breathing, to pressing their nail bed to cause pain and thus a reaction if they are alive, to placing a raw onion below someone's nose in the hope of a reaction to the smell (Doig, 2022).

After death, the body begins immediately to undergo processes of decomposition. The death of the physical body is therefore precursor to further change, which involves movement and flux as the body breaks down and eventually, without the interference of other humans, it will become part of the earth (Alfsdotter & Petaros, 2021). There are a number of stages through which the decomposing body must go, some of which will be discussed in Chapter 5.

Impact of Technology

There are occasions when human actions impact processes of dying, death and decay, through the utilisation of technologies which delay death or obscure the fact of its occurrence. Such occasions may include, for example, cases where a person is kept by the application of technology in a new and altered state of consciousness. After a severe brain injury, an individual may experience a disorder of consciousness which can result in them being maintained, through the intervention of medical technology, in a minimally conscious state, where the person shows occasional signs of awareness. In some instances, it is also possible that someone may be in a vegetative state, in which the person gives no signs of awareness at all (Kitzinger & Kitzinger, 2014). This technology may stave off death for an extended period of time, during which the person's body is still warm, but they display no apparent consciousness. This seeming contradiction makes it difficult for families to negotiate their way through the experience and decide whether they feel that their person is dead or alive (Kitzinger & Kitzinger, 2014).

Situations such as being in a permanent vegetative state appear to place the individual in a liminal space between being alive and being dead. They may sometimes be regarded as a person who retains agency but at others as an object without personhood; the ways in which they are perceived and treated shift, sometimes from moment to moment, depending upon who is the observer (Bird-David & Israeli, 2010).

People in these states of minimal consciousness may have their bodies kept alive through the use of advanced medical technology, and sometimes this may continue for years. There are occasions when treatment which has been sustaining life in the person's body is withdrawn in order to facilitate the transplantation of organs to save the life of someone else. While it is the case that there are far fewer donors of organs for transplant than there is need, on a global basis, the process of withdrawing technology from one person to save another is replete with emotional, ethical, technical and logistical issues (Smith et al., 2019). As noted by Dr Hamilton, there may be energy left in a body's cells even after the point of no return has been reached, such that the person whose body it was is irretrievably deceased. However, when their body has been maintained in a lifelike appearance through technological interventions, it can be difficult for their families and friends to comprehend that there is no possibility that they will recover and pick up their life as it was when they were injured (Kitzinger & Kitzinger, 2014).

The way in which organ donation is managed varies by country (Smith et al., 2019). In all countries of the United Kingdom, there is an opt-out system whereby if an individual does not wish their organs to be donated after death, they can register this. Otherwise, there is the expectation that their organs may be donated after they have died, with the proviso that their family can prevent this from happening. The most recent UK nation to move to an opt-out system is Northern Ireland, with the change being implemented on 1 June 2023 under what is known as Dáithí's Law.[5]

Technology also enables the moment of a death to be relocated from a troubling public space to one deemed more suitable for the occurrence of death. Automated external defibrillators are now situated in many public spaces in the United Kingdom for members of the public to use in the case of a perceived cardiac arrest (Kulakiewicz & Balogun, 2021). A study of this technology's use found that on occasion, those using the defibrillator realised that the person had died but continued trying to revive them until such time as the body could be removed to a more private space, such as an ambulance. Research participants had made the decision to appear as if they were still trying to revive the person they knew had died so that a troubling death could be taken out of the public place where it had no business to be into a healthcare site where deaths are supposed to occur and away from the public gaze (Timmons et al., 2010).

Technological means are also sometimes used in a deliberate effort to increase an individual's lifespan or to ensure their immortality after their body's biological death. Possibilities are, for example, opting for cryogenic preservation, using the most up-to-date anti-ageing treatments, or choosing to freeze one's eggs for future

---

[5]Human Tissue Authority, Deceased organ and tissue donation for transplants, https://www.hta.gov.uk/guidance-public/body-organ-and-tissue-donation/deceased-organ-and-tissue-donation-transplants
NI Direct, Organ donation, https://www.nidirect.gov.uk/articles/organ-donation

parenthood and the maintenance of one's genetic heritage (Bozzaro, 2022; Dein, 2022).

Such technologically inspired situations are potentially troubling in relation to time of death. The notion of death as occurring in a moment of time, as the concept is often understood, no longer seems viable, given the ways in which death can be hidden, sometimes be deferred or delayed or appear to be deferred. Yet any deferring of death can only be temporary, and the means by which the extension is procured may be somewhat costly in terms of time and physical and emotional pain (Bozzaro, 2022).

Usual Deaths

The WHO is an agency of the United Nations, and it has 194 member states. Its remit is to focus on the creation of a world which is healthier and safer for its human inhabitants. Among the many other tasks which the WHO takes on, it produces an International Classification of Diseases (ICD), the most recent version of which, number 11, came into effect at the start of 2022 (World Health Organization, 2023a). The WHO divides causes of death into three separate categories. The first category is communicable diseases, which includes infectious and parasitic diseases and maternal, perinatal and nutritional conditions, the second is noncommunicable, or chronic, diseases and the third category is of injuries (World Health Organization, 2020). In 2019, globally seven out of the 10 main causes of death were chronic diseases such as heart disease, strokes, cancers, diabetes and Alzheimer's disease. The numbers of people dying from chronic disease are increasing over time, while the numbers who die from infectious diseases are decreasing, although it is worth noting that the burden of deaths from communicable diseases is greater in the world's least wealthy countries (World Health Organization, 2020).

The most common death in the United Kingdom in the 21st century is that of an older person, and it often occurs after a period of declining health. In 2021, 586,334 deaths were registered in England and Wales. Of these deaths, COVID-19 was listed as underlying cause in 11.5% of deaths, which made it the leading cause. The other leading causes were dementia and Alzheimer's disease, ischaemic heart diseases, cerebrovascular diseases and malignant neoplasm of trachea, bronchus and lung (Office for National Statistics, 2022b). COVID-19, as a communicable disease, has shifted the balance of the leading causes of death in England and Wales which, prior to the start of the 2020 pandemic, were predominantly non-communicable diseases. In 2013, the majority of deaths were of older people, with 91% of female deaths and 86% of male deaths being of people over the age of 60 (Office for National Statistics, 2014). While younger people die, and from a range of causes, this is relatively rare in England and Wales in the 21st century.

Deaths of this kind which are experienced by most people are subject to certain procedures once they have taken place. This includes the recording of when they happened as well as the cause, and the United Kingdom has a legal system which requires every death to be recorded. The way in which countries manage the deaths of their populations varies, although the WHO does make recommendations as to how this process should be handled, including a recommended template for a certificate of the cause of death and a guide as to how the certificate should be completed (World Health Organization, 2023b).[6] This will be explored further in Chapter 5.

Not all deaths are like this, however. There are also deaths which occur suddenly and unexpectedly, through accident or which are caused by the actions of the person who dies or someone else.

Assisted Dying

Assisted dying is the process by which someone who wishes to end their life does so with the assistance of another person. In some countries, such as Canada, New Zealand, Switzerland, Belgium, Netherlands, Australia, Luxembourg and some states of the United States of America, it is legal for a medical professional to assist with the death of a person. There are rules which limit those who are eligible for assisted dying, for example, whether only those who have a diagnosed terminal illness can access it, and there are also regulations about how it should be carried out and whether the individual must be able to administer the lethal medication themselves. There are other countries which are discussing the possibility of legislation to allow assisted dying, for example, Spain, Germany, Scotland and England (BMA, 2023; Mroz et al., 2020).[7]

At the start of 2023, assisted dying is illegal in all four nations of the United Kingdom. This means that voluntary euthanasia, by which one person ends another's life when asked to do so by the person who wishes to die, is against the law, as is assisted suicide by which one person provides the means for another to kill themselves (Richards, 2017). One result of this ongoing illegality for people in the United Kingdom is that a new practice of suicide tourism has arisen, by which terminally ill people travel to Switzerland where it is legal, under certain circumstances, for foreigners to visit so that they can be assisted to die (Richards, 2017).

The issue of assisted dying is one which prompts strong feelings, and there are organisations in the United Kingdom which campaign for its introduction into law, and there are other organisations which campaign for it to remain illegal. The key point here is that when an individual undergoes an assisted death, it is planned to take place at a specific day and time. This, too, will be revisited in Chapter 5.

---

[6]WHO, 2022, Mortality database resources: International form of medical certificate of cause of death, https://platform.who.int/mortality/resources
[7]British Medical Association, 2021, Physician Assisted Dying: https://www.bma.org.uk/advice-and-support/ethics/end-of-life/physician-assisted-dying

Socially Proscribed Deaths

Proscribed deaths are an important lens through which to consider time of death and what it means, by comparing and contrasting with the ways in which usual deaths are noted and recorded in relation to when they occurred. There are various ways in which people can die proscribed deaths, but here we will consider only two: dying alone at home and genocide and deaths caused through crimes against humanity. These examples have been chosen as they will make differing contributions to the discussion of the concept time of death.

Genocide/Crimes Against Humanity

The United Nations has an Office on Genocide Prevention and the Responsibility to Protect, which was established in an effort to prevent the occurrence of genocide and other crimes against humanity and also to raise awareness of the issues involved.[8] Genocide was recognised as an international crime in 1946 by the UN General Assembly. As of 2018, 149 states had ratified the United Nations' 1948 Genocide Convention, although the International Criminal Court has stated that it is not necessary for a state to ratify the convention in order to be liable for prosecution under its provisions. The Court considers that the Convention 'embodies principles that are part of general customary international law'. Genocide is defined as carrying out an act with the intention of destroying all or some members of a national, ethnic, racial or religious group. This can be done by killing people, causing harm to them as individuals, imposing living conditions inimical to their survival, forcibly removing children from the group or taking steps to prevent births among members of the group. Such acts can take place during war or peace. Crimes against humanity involve acts against a civilian population and can include murder, torture, forced imprisonment, enslavement, forced disappearance, apartheid, rape and other forms of sexual violence (International Criminal Court, 2011).

Shaw (2012) suggests that genocide is a crime of social classification, in which those with power target those without power and destroy them, either physically or socially. Such crimes are not usually committed by individual murderers, and they often involve state sanctioned actors from different sectors (Williams & Pfeiffer, 2017). Crimes against humanity and genocide have occurred in many parts of the world, including Germany, Cambodia, Rwanda, Chile, Argentina, Armenia, Cyprus, the Balkans and Spain. When killing is involved in such crimes, little regard is paid by perpetrators to the respectful disposal of the dead body and the informing of family members about what has happened. Indeed, the murderers' concern may be rather to conceal what has happened, and bodies may be hidden in mass, unmarked graves so that families are left without knowing what happened to their person.

---

[8]United Nations Office on Genocide Prevention and the Responsibility to Protect, https://www.un.org/en/genocideprevention/index.shtml

As time passes, however, and there are changes in governments and the holders of power in the different geographical locations, attempts have been made to find and identify the bodies of those who have been killed and lost. Efforts have been, and are, made '... to determine the numbers, identities, and cause of death of victims of state crimes and violent conflict, return their bodies to family members, and contribute evidence to legal trials for crimes such as crimes against humanity, genocide, torture, and enforced disappearance' (Moon, 2019, p. 39). Such crimes are horrendous and shocking. People who are killed in such a way are treated as non-persons, and their bodies are buried or otherwise disposed of with scant regard for their humanity. The fate of their bodies at the time of their deaths will be revisited in Chapter 5 as part of the examination of how the time of death can be measured.

Dying Alone

Every year in the United Kingdom, there are an unknown number of deaths where the person who died lived alone, died while alone at home and where their body was undiscovered for an extended period of time. Increasing numbers of people, at all adult ages, are living alone, and geographical mobility means that many older people live far away from family members. Living alone does not, however, mean that an individual lacks social contacts. Some people live alone and have active lives, giving them plenty of social contact so that they have good support networks and are part of their local communities. However, there are some people who isolate themselves from the wider community and who prefer to live a solitary life. In some instances, the isolation into which they retreat is so severe that they may be described as entering a period of self-imposed social death. In such a case, it is possible for the individual to die at home and for no one to notice their absence from the world. When this happens, their body is likely to be discovered when entry is forced into their home for some reason not associated with their death. I term such an occurrence a lone death. This is in order to distinguish it from the situation where someone dies while alone at home, but they are then missed from their usual activities so that someone takes steps to seek them out and so discovers that they have died (Caswell, 2022). A lone death opens another perspective on the concept of time of death, which will be considered in Chapter 5.

Grief Responses to Death

Death often prompts an emotional reaction in humans. This may be one of fear or anxiety in relation to their own future demise, or it may be a grief response to the death of another person. We tend to think of emotions as being individual and personal. Emotion is felt at a personal level, and that feeling is experienced whether or not we are able to articulate it to ourselves or share the experience with others. This may seem to put emotion beyond the reach of observation, yet research reveals that there is a social side to emotion and its expression; how, for example, do we give a name to our feelings, how do we show what we are feeling or how do we know what is an appropriate emotion to feel in a given situation (Bericat, 2016)? Emotions may be felt towards other people or prompted by their actions, socially appropriate emotional expression may also be learned from interactions with others and engaged in through a desire not to behave outwith the social norms (van Kleef et al., 2016).

Grief is an emotional response to loss which is believed to be a universal human experience and one which is influenced by the social setting within which the individual lives (Ang, 2023; Walter, 1999). How any one person experiences and expresses their grief will vary so that the landscape of grief is multidimensional 'and shaped by social, cultural, historical, and political factors' (Silverman et al., 2021, p. 1). Within this landscape are to be found many ways of expressing and experiencing grief which yet hold common social roots. Individuals learn how they should grieve, and what is considered appropriate behaviour in their community (Walter, 1999).

The social shaping of grief experiences highlights the fact that practices and ideas about them change. For example, a funeral which celebrates the life of the deceased person is a common place in the United Kingdom, yet it would once have been unknown, and maintaining an ongoing relationship with someone who has died would once have been perceived as a sign of illness, but this is no longer the case (Walter, 1999). When someone has undergone a bereavement, it is not unusual for them to seek meaning in relation to the death by looking beyond themselves to their wider community. They may campaign for change or endeavour to raise funds for research into a specific kind of dying or to provide care and support for others in a similar situation. It is also possible that this wider community of family, friends, colleagues, neighbours, acquaintances and even strangers may monitor the way in which the bereaved person enacts their grief (Neimeyer et al., 2014).[9]

Conclusion

People know that they are going to die if they allow themselves to think about it. Each person dies not once but twice. Their body will die when it ceases to function and passes the point of irreversibility so that there is no return for them as the person they were. Their body will then begin to decompose. They will also undergo a social death, when they cease to have any degree of agency in the world. Processes of change are integral to both kinds of dying. The dying body changes and continues to change after decease. Social death is also a matter of changes which occur in the relationships which the individual has with other people and the impact which they have on the lives of others. The dying of one

---

[9]There is a wide range of literature available on bereavement, grief and mourning. A good starting point from which to engage with this literature is, I think, Tony Walter's book *On Bereavement*.

individual prompts changes for those close to them, socially, psychologically, emotionally and also on a practical level.

When a person's body dies, there is an immediate absence. For those closely bereaved by the death, there is no longer a living, breathing, talking, thinking person to interact with. The body must be managed in such a way as to protect those living from the sensory experience of bodily decay. The bereaved may continue to think of the person as if they were still alive, however, and take account of their perceived wishes, ideas, opinions and beliefs. In such a manner, an individual with no bodily existence may be afforded some measure of agency in the world and so remain socially alive for a period.

The idea that change is integral to death and that each person dies twice, once in a biological and once in a social sense, will be taken forward for discussion in relation to the concept time of death. The next chapter explores some aspects of time in relation to death.

Chapter 4

Time and Death

Introduction

Death does not seem to make sense without the limits set on life by time, for humans live out their lives in a temporal, as well as geographical, space. People are born, live and then die in time and space (Schick, 2022). The aim of this chapter is to bring together the two concepts of time and death, as they have been discussed in the previous two chapters. This is so that they can be used to address the book's overall aim of exploring the concept of time of death from a sociological perspective and asking the question 'when is the time of death?'

   Time, as we understand and use it, is a social construct. Whether we believe that it works in a linear or cyclical manner it fits with the idea of beginnings and endings, with what appears to be the observable fact that all living creatures are born, grow, age and die. Indeed, all living things do so, including plants. Their life cycle may be measured in days or centuries, but growth, change and death are ever present.

   The lives of living creatures, including humans, are subject to change and must end in death; living beings on earth are not immortal. But even after death the change continues through processes of decay and decomposition. The language of time is deeply embedded in ideas about processes of dying and what happens to bodies after the death of the individual and this makes it very difficult, if not impossible, to speak about human lives and human dying, without recourse also to the language of time.

   Chapter 2 suggested that while the nature of time may not be understood, one key facet of it is that it is a social construct and, as such, individuals and groups use it as a way of organising the experiences and the events in their lives. Within any social setting there are shared understandings of how time works within that context, and this means that individuals can communicate with each other effectively on issues which have temporal sensitivity. This facilitates the efficient operation of systems which enable individuals to work, play, socialise, travel, care for each other and to carry out many other activities which form part of 21st century life. These activities include the range of processes around dying and its aftermath.

   Chapter 3 argued that dying is a process and that change is integral to the process. Bodies undergo continual changes throughout their lives. A body's cells

Time of Death, 47–57
Copyright © 2024 Glenys Caswell
Published under exclusive licence by Emerald Publishing Limited
doi:10.1108/978-1-80455-005-220241004

constantly die and are replaced, although probably without the individual's awareness, and processes of ageing occur along the life course. Disease may affect a body at any stage and sometimes this will lead to the death of the biological entity. Change continues after the death of the organism, as processes of decay and decomposition take hold. Dying also involves social change in terms of human experience and relationships, both for the person who dies and those who know and care about them.

This chapter aims to bring together the concepts of time and death, through the consideration of time as an organising concept as a way of making sense of the change processes involved in dying and death. It first discusses mortality awareness and time, then experiencing time towards the end of a life. It goes on to discuss biological death and time, death deferring technologies and time, social death and time and death and liminal time. The chapter ends by looking at time of death as a social construction.

Mortality Awareness and Time

In his work, *Being and Time*, '...Heidegger proposes being-towards-death as the basis for understanding the temporal structure of human existence. As people reckon explicitly or inexplicitly with their finitude, he argues, they invest their lives with significance and appreciate how that significance relates to the worlds in which they live' (Nielsen & Skotnicki, 2019, p. 112). This suggests that it is possible for individuals to be aware of their mortality and to use this awareness as a way of imbuing their lives with meaning; for some people, having limited time can promote a feeling of purpose in life.

Baert et al. (2022) suggest that people often arrange their lives around existential milestones. Attainment of these milestones, which may include such things as having a long-term partnership and family or becoming established in a career, help to give individuals a sense of achievement and purpose. The sense of the value of reaching a milestone is one that is shared among the social group, so that the achievement is recognised by others and is cause for celebration (Bauman, 2005; Baert et al., 2022). Turner (2022) reminds us that the milestones which individuals aim for as they move further into the 21st century are more variable than they perhaps were in the past and that not all are open to everyone. Following a chronological route through the lifespan, starting with education and followed by work, marriage and children, ending inevitably in retirement is no longer the invariable pattern. Sometimes, mature adults enter education as a student, individuals may have portfolio working careers which involve moving from one sphere of activity to another, and not everyone chooses to enter a long-term relationship. What is inevitable, however, is death at the end of life. There is an expectation that this will be when the person has reached an advanced age, and that is usually the case, although people at all ages from the newly born onwards may die.

Time links the events and experiences in people's lives, whether they follow a socially expected path or choose their own way through life. When looking back to the past and the experiences they have had, they can place them in order and see links between them, whether temporal or not. They can look ahead and know that the future holds their demise although, unless they have been given a diagnosis of terminal illness, it is unlikely that they will have any knowledge of when this will occur.

Individuals in the 21st century generally have a longer life expectancy than those in any other previous century. For many people today, the longer life that they have is lived with better health and in improved conditions. Despite this, some people may wish to live longer lives, or to appear young for a longer period, and this may prompt them to engage in the use of medical technologies which promise to defer ageing processes (Bozzaro, 2022).

Experiencing Time Towards the End of a Life

When an individual is given a diagnosis of terminal illness from a medical professional the kinds of information that they wish to receive will vary. Some will want to know how much time they have left before they will die, although it is unlikely that the physician will be able to say with any certainty how long that will be. Other people may prefer not to know how much longer they have to live (Reith & Payne, 2009). Kellehear (2014) suggests that some people who know that they are dying may attain a completely new sense of time. He describes the experience of one woman who, by listening to the words of her young child, comes to discover the notion of timelessness as a real possibility; a second can be or seem to be an eternity (Kellehear, 2014, pp. 214–215).

Research exploring people's experiences of time during the terminal phase of their illness found that their temporal perceptions may change relative to the period when they were ill but not acknowledged as terminally ill. The speed of time passing altered during the terminal phase and, for some participants, it could change almost on a day to day basis. Most deliberately lived one day at a time and did not plan for the future. For a proportion of participants, the past had become the dominant time period as it was known and safe, rather than the future which was foreshortened and riven with uncertainty (Rovers et al., 2019).

Time, for people approaching the end of life, may also be experienced as if it were suspended. Individuals in this situation will not necessarily think of themselves as waiting to die, but for them the present endures and stretches ahead. Research participants with chronic illness who were approaching the end of their lives described how, for them, '...the past and the future receded; only the present moment was important' (Sacks & Nelson, 2007, p. 685). Participants created for themselves an 'emotional space' where their suffering did not matter and in which they were suspended effectively out of time (Sacks & Nelson, 2007, p. 685). Research suggests that some people who are diagnosed with a terminal illness reframe their view of the future and create hope for themselves in a way which is consistent with their limited time. They may set goals for themselves, such as creating a legacy for those who are bereaved by their death through the setting up of a memory box, containing mementoes of their lives together, or they might aim to attend the wedding of a significant person in their lives (Garrard & Wrigley, 2009; Johnson, 2007). While, to an outsider, this may look like waiting, for the person themselves, rather than waiting for death, the reframing brings hope and a more purposive approach to their remaining life.

When someone is in the terminal phase of an illness there may be treatment offered which does not promise a cure but holds out the allure of deferring their death so that they have more time to be spent with family and friends and to do the things that the dying person wants to do. The promise of more time presumes that, for at least some of that time, the person will feel well and strong enough to engage with the people around them and to carry out their desired activities. There are, however, also potential downsides to this. For example, it is possible that undergoing the treatment which potentially offers extra time may require the person to be in hospital for longer than would otherwise be the case. It is also possible that accepting such treatment can result in side effects which are detrimental to the person's feeling of well-being and their ability to do as they would wish. Such a situation has been described by oncologists as 'time toxicity', where the desired additional time turns out to be toxic, rather than beneficial, for the dying person (Gupta et al., 2022).

Time may also be experienced differently for people close to someone with a terminal illness. Research with people who had cared for a dying relative and were bereaved suggests that, for them, time no longer passes in a linear fashion. After the death, participants found that they may alternate between having so much to do in terms of administrative work relating to the death and its aftermath and having too much time with nothing to do other than reflect on their experience and feelings. While reflection was an important part of their grieving, suddenly having time on their hands to manage after sometimes extended periods of caring for their dying person was difficult. There was also a tension for some between doing their grieving in their own way and own time, and what they perceived to be the socially and culturally approved ways of doing grief (Kenny et al., 2019).

The enactment of time in institutional settings where people die, such as hospices, hospitals or care homes, is an amalgam of personally experienced time alongside the temporal rhythms and patterns required to keep the institution functioning efficiently (Zerubavel, 1981). Staff working in a Dutch hospice are regulated by the clock, for example, in the setting of the start and end of shifts, but patients operate to their own, idiosyncratic schedules. They wake and sleep, eat, get up and engage with others when they choose to do so. Most patients die in the hospice, often staying towards the end of their lives in their room and at this point time is controlled by their bodily needs and processes. Patients manage time in different ways. Some engage in processes of absenting themselves from the past and their previous relationships, perhaps as a way of preparing themselves for what is to come. Some patients prepare plans for a future they will not have, but this does not necessarily mean that they are denying the imminence of their death it is, rather, a technique to handle time which they know is limited (Pasveer, 2019).

Zivkovic (2018) proposes the concept of temporal dissonance, which posits the idea that people who try to plan for their future care at the end of life may experience a disjuncture in attempting to put themselves ahead of time. The idea of advance care planning is to set out wishes and plans for care when a person is approaching the end of life and is perhaps in a position where they cannot speak for themselves. One of the difficulties in doing such planning is that, however careful the planner may be in articulating and setting out their wishes, they cannot include everything which may occur because the future is unknown. So, what they are doing is to agree some options while simultaneously shutting off access to others. By trying to plan for an uncertain future, people are putting themselves and their families in a position where they may well experience a disconnection between what they want or need when the time for care comes and what they have requested in advance (Zivkovic, 2018).

Advance care planning is not the only process which may lead people into the experience of temporal dissonance. The decision to consider utilising the right to assisted dying, for example, may also place individuals in a space of temporal dissonance, as they weigh up their options. For people living in the United Kingdom who wish to have an assisted death, it is necessary to travel abroad as such a death is illegal in the United Kingdom. As noted in Chapter 3, each year people travel to Switzerland to access an assisted death, which is guaranteed to be effective and painless. In order to die in Switzerland, they must take time to plan and provide the necessary evidence of their status to the clinic they opt for.[1] When starting to plan, individuals are wishing '...to transcend their current or future suffering', but they are placing themselves ahead of time and trying to understand how they will feel when the time comes (Richards, 2017, p. 358).

Planning for the future is a process that humans engage with, trying to cast themselves forward in time and imagine how they wish their life to be and how they can achieve that wish. They do this in many spheres of existence, from career planning to deciding where to live and who to live with. But when attempting to imagine their future dying and death the process can be charged with emotion as they endeavour to work out what will be the best for them. The risk is that they will situate themselves in what turns out to be a space of temporal dissonance, such that when the time comes for them to require end of life care or an assisted death, they find that what they had expected to want or need no longer meets what their unexpected future self requires. We have little understanding of how people who are dying experience time, and thus lack the ability to help others look ahead and plan for their future dying in a way that matches their likely future temporal understanding and experience.

---

[1]For example, Dignitas is the most well-known organisation which caters for people from the United Kingdom: http://www.dignitas.ch/?lang=en
There are others, however, such as the Pegasos Swiss Association: https://pegasos-association.com/ and the Life Circle Clinic: https://www.lifecircle.ch/en/?no_cache=1

Biological Death and Time

To answer the question 'when is the time of death' it is necessary to understand the perspective of the person asking, and the purpose behind the question, for there are many possible answers. If the query relates to the dying of the biological organism that is a human being, then it is possible that the answer requires a response that alludes to the calendar and the clock. The exact time is not always easy to determine, unless a trained observer watches the dying person, armed with an accurate timepiece and then records the precise moment that the person's body stops living. It would be difficult to accomplish this in the case of most deaths, and it is not usually deemed necessary to record such a precise time of death. The one circumstance when accuracy is deemed desirable, however, is in forensic cases.

When a person is killed by another person there will be an investigation, one element of which is a forensic post-mortem. What this does is to determine the cause of death and it also attempts to establish the 'time death interval', the period between the death and the discovery of the body, as accurately as possible (Black, 2018). The effort to establish how long it is since the individual died will involve observation and recording of changes to the body. However, that is not straightforward as many factors speed up or slow down bodily decomposition, and these need to be taken into account in the post-mortem process (Black, 2018; Shrestha et al., 2021).

Pathologists have an array of techniques and skills to utilise in attempting to refine the time death interval, and research continues to identify ever more accurate techniques. Work is ongoing, for example, into examining the use of insect activity on corpses, the exploration of the use of circadian biomarkers, and the analysis of potassium in the vitreous eye fluid, among other methods (Matuszewski, 2021; Sibbens et al., 2017; Zilg et al., 2015).

Away from the world of post-mortems and murder investigations, what does it mean to ask when a death occurred? Today, many countries have a legal requirement for deaths to be certified and registered, and although processes vary considerably the cause of death is generally needed. In the United Kingdom, the law requires that each death be registered and the responsibility for this devolves upon individuals who are identified within the legislation, and who will often be a relative of the deceased person.[2] Further, not to register a death within the specified time period, of eight days in Scotland and five days in the rest of the United Kingdom, is a criminal offence.[3] Before a relative is able to register a death, they will need to have received a copy of the death certificate, which must be signed by a medical professional. The English death certificate has a space for the date of death as reported to the medical practitioner completing the form and which will be noted by the registrar when the death is subsequently registered

---

[2]Bereavement Advice Centre, 'Who can register a death?': https://www.bereavement advice.org/topics/registering-a-death-and-informing-others/who-can-register-a-death/
[3]Blackstone Solicitors, 'What happens if you don't register a death within five days?', 2021: https://blackstonesolicitorsltd.co.uk/category/news/what-happens-if-you-dont-register-a-death-within-5-days/

(Millares-Martin, 2020). This appears to offer a calendrical time of death although, as will be explored in Chapter 5, this is not so straightforward as it may at first appear.

The moment of death has been deemed one of significance through much of history, with people who are emotionally close to a dying person believing that this is an important moment for them to witness and a time when they should accompany their person (Donnelly & Donnelly, 2006). Rée (2017) explores peoples' interest in the moment of death, through an engagement with literary sources, such as Leo Tolstoy and Charles Dickens. He suggests that, as individuals who will also die one day, we have this fact in common and it therefore fascinates us to witness death; we can identify with the dying because one day that will be us (Rée, 2017, p. 135).

Research in the 21st century suggests that the moment of death is perceived by those close to the dying person as an intimate moment, and one which their family and friends are keen to witness, even though this may involve a lot of effort. This witnessing occurs through the enactment of a vigil at the bedside of the dying person, which may comprise one or more people, and at which a variety of activities may take place. These activities can include reading or talking to the dying person, praying, chatting as a familial group, laughing, eating and drinking, sitting quietly or holding the person's hand. Despite the attendance of the family it often happens that they will miss the moment of the death, either because they have temporarily left the bedside or because they had failed to realise that the death had taken place (e.g. Caswell et al., 2022; Donnelly & Battley, 2010; Donnelly & Donnelly, 2006; Kellehear, 2013; Valentine, 2007).

Instances where the person dies during the period when they have been left alone have led some to believe that people may have a measure of choice in when they die, and that they may choose to die so that their family are saved the pain of the moment, or because being alone means that they no longer feel tethered to life (Caswell & O'Connor, 2019). There have also been suggestions, anecdotally, that sometimes people will delay their dying until a significant date is reached. For example, for some individuals the desire to live long enough to see the anniversary of a parent's death, or witness an adult child's wedding, may motivate them to delay their death (Dein & George, 2001). The notion that dying people are able to exercise agency in relation to when they die is familiar at the level of the stories that we tell ourselves and each other, but there is little evidence of its reality. One obvious way in which terminally ill individuals may attain some control over both the manner and timing of their deaths is through an assisted death, although this is not an easy option and is particularly difficult for individuals living in countries where assisted dying is illegal (Richards, 2017). Having analysed the number of burials taking place at Dan Dolo Cemetery in Kano, Nigeria, Last (2013) cautiously suggests that some members of a long established Muslim community are able to will themselves to die on a Friday, the most auspicious day of the week.

Attempting to answer the when of a death is thus not straightforward, and it takes many words and the work of many disciplines, including the sciences, social sciences, arts and humanities. Parsons (2017), for example, takes a historical approach examining the fear and risk of premature burial in 1830s Britain. At the time, there was no established system for certifying that a person was dead before they were placed in their coffin and buried, and the Registration of Births and Deaths Act 1836 did not require a physician to see a body before signing a death certificate. It is perhaps not surprising, therefore, that some people were afraid the timing of deaths might be mistaken (Parsons, 2017, pp. 70–71).

Death Deferring Technology and Time

As noted in Chapter 3, there are technologies available in the 21st century which can delay the deaths of individuals. People may be kept in a minimally conscious or vegetative state, sometimes for long periods of time (Kitzinger & Kitzinger, 2014). Technology can also be used to hide the fact that a death has occurred and move it into a more suitable geographical and temporal space (Timmons et al., 2010). These are both examples of temporal manipulation. Death may be hidden from public view, or the death of an individual may be deferred from now until a later time, obscuring the real time of its occurrence. There is a resonance here with the actions of Christie's Dr James Sheppard who murdered Roger Ackroyd despite the difference in motivations and the differing technologies available (Christie, 1926/2007).

Social Death and Time

Social death was discussed in Chapter 3. To undergo a process of social death results in a person lacking agency such that they are no longer an active social agent in the lives of others (Mulkay & Ernst, 1991). This form of death can occur prior to the body's death, at the same time as biological death, or at a time later than when the body dies. In most cases, it is impossible to tell when such a death has occurred, given that there is not an embodied presence in the world to demonstrate the social existence of the individual. However, occasionally a dead body will be found in circumstances which reveal a person who had been unnoticed by the wider world and who had therefore been socially deceased prior to their biological death (Caswell, 2022).

The time of a social death cannot be categorised by the clock or the calendar but already, in speaking of it in relation to biological death, we are using temporal language to situate it. That is, we are saying that it happens before, at the same time as, or after biological death, and these are all words used to ascribe temporal relationships. Social death is not visible and it is usually unknowable, and we can only use descriptive temporal language and relate it to other occurrences, such as the death of the physical organism. Further consideration will be given to this in Chapters 5 and 7.

Death and Liminal Time

For individuals who are occupying a liminal time they are in a position of ambiguity, they are '...neither here nor there; they are betwixt and between...' (Turner, 1969, p. 95). Dying people and those around them are likely to be in a liminal time – not dead yet, but no longer fully integrated into the world of the living. When the people who care about them are waiting, hoping and yet knowing that the only outcome is a death they are in the liminal time which exists between being a partner and a widow, between being a friend and a bereaved friend.

Writing about funerals, Hogue (2006) uses travel as a metaphor to aid readers in getting to grips with the concept of liminality:

> The image of physical travel further helps us make sense of the "in-between-ness" we experience when we are in transit in the cycle of life; we feel ourselves at a threshold and sense that we are neither here nor yet there. Indeed, the Latin word limen (for threshold) is the root word for liminal time or space, that is, time outside of time or in between times. (Hogue, 2006, p. 4)

Time of death is a liminal time for those who are emotionally invested in a dying. Those who will be bereaved are in between having the person as an embodied presence in their lives and the time when their person has moved onto the world of the dead and when they have integrated the embodied absence into their view of the world. How long a bereaved individual will remain in this liminal temporal space will vary. Dying people are in a place that is between being an embodied presence in the world and being deceased, a dead body, an ancestor. Thus all who are emotionally involved in the dying of an individual are in a status of ambiguity, whether as dying person or about-to-be bereaved person.

Research with people with cancer who attended an outpatient clinic and who were in receipt of palliative care found that they were not so much in liminal time, in between living and dying, but were rather in what the authors describe as a parallax state. The people whom the researchers interviewed were not simply passively existing in a state of limbo between life and death, but they were both living and dying. They moved between sites of care and treatment and their personal and social lives, making choices and being active social agents. They were people with lives still to live, not merely patients of the healthcare system (MacArtney et al., 2015).

The time of death, the time at which a person dies, is sometimes ambiguous. It may be that their family members who are present do not realise that they have died it may be that they were alone at the moment of decease and their body was not found until a short time later. However it may come about, it is possible that the death in these cases took place in a liminal temporal space, and that they were neither dead nor alive until their companions became aware of their decease. This will be discussed further in the next two chapters.

Time of Death as a Social Construction

Whether time exists or not, we live as if it does. It seems likely that time is not as we tend to think of it, that it is not something which runs in linear fashion but is relative and depends upon where you are and how fast you are moving. It is also possible that it is not fixed but in flux. Or perhaps time as we think of it does not exist at all (Barron et al., 2022), and the world is a collection of events, rather than minutes and days, and one where objects are perpetually in motion (Rovelli, 2017; Nail, 2022). When we talk of our experiences of time, we may be referring to motion, to events and to things happening and how we experience the passage of events, of life in motion. We call it time as a shorthand way of referring to the constant flux and change of life and how we experience it. This is the social construction of time, the way in which we have built a concept of time that fits with the societies in which we live, but also allows us to have divergent experiences which do not fit with our society's temporal norms (Berger & Luckman, 1967; Luckman, 1991).

The concept time of death is discussed here within the context of a social milieu where the nature of time is not understood, but where its existence is assumed. We believe that we know time through its effects, which seem to be explicitly apparent in processes of change and we have developed socially and culturally dependent time narratives as a way of integrating time into human lives. This leaves us in a situation where '...the issue of whether time is separable from change – from events – or whether it is in some sense the product of events, remains unresolved' (Tallis, 2016).

Data in this book come from research conducted mainly in England, thus situating temporal understandings and beliefs in those of the global north. The time narrative here is of linear time encompassing the past, the present and the future, where the past is finished (except in memory and imagination) and the future unknowable (except through prediction and waiting). It is possible, however, that within this social context people's experience of time may contradict the linear narrative.

Sophisticated systems have been developed to keep track of, and record, time and these shared ways of measuring passing time permit the chronicity and organisation of social life (Zerubavel, 1981). For individuals in the 21st century, the measuring and recording of time give an illusion of control over it. The mistaken idea that we can control time is most notable in the case of death, as time and death appear inextricably linked through processes of change evident in the dying, decay and decomposition of the human body. For those who are emotionally involved with the dying and death of a particular person, this period is one of liminality and ambiguity as they are 'betwixt and between' life and death, living and dying.

Conclusion

In this exploration of the concept 'time of death', time is a social construction which individuals and groups use to organise their experiences and the events that occur in the social world around them. This includes the ways in which experiences around dying and death occur. Just as change is an integral part of death, so time is a way of arranging experiences which assist people to understand what is happening. Individuals in a social context are well versed in the ways in which time is used and applies in different situations. It is also the case that powerful groups, whether governments or those with access to particular kinds of social capital, can utilise time as a tool to exercise power (Nowotny, 1994).

The next two chapters take the discussion about time of death forward, by presenting empirical data from the two research projects described earlier. Chapter 5 engages with the topic of measuring the time of death, and this is followed by a chapter which considers what it means to experience the time of death, particularly when you care about the person who dies.

Chapter 5

Measuring Time of Death

Introduction

This chapter engages with the human endeavour to measure, and record, time of death. This effort appears to go to the heart of the question 'when is the time of death?' by focusing on the biological death of the body. Recording the time of death is a mainly institutional endeavour, and the institutions involved, such as the state and legal system, are not concerned with social death but only with biological death. Since the 19th century, systems have been developed in the United Kingdom for the monitoring of the births and deaths of individual members of society (Higgs, 2004). Data that are recorded about deaths have changed over time, but in the 21st century, this includes when a death occurred, as well as who it was that died and the cause. It is certainly the case that a dying body requires attention, and the death of the body leaves behind a decomposing corpse which needs to be dealt with, both for the sake of public health and also for the enactment of the social duties of the living to the dead (Howarth, 2007).

The meaning of the phrase 'time of death' may appear self-evident, and the dearth of social scientific studies examining the concept supports this assumption. A range of medical research projects continue the attempt to find more accurate ways to pinpoint the time of death, but there has been little effort so far in the social science community to explore what is meant by the phrase 'time of death'.

This chapter contains both literature and the presentation of empirical data in the process of exploring how we go about attempting to measure the time of a person's biological death. As has already been noted, the process of social death tends not to be amenable to measurement, and it will therefore be included in the next chapter. The aim here is to tease out what we know about the ways in which time of death is measured and recorded and also to think about the possible reasons behind these attempts. The empirical data, which speak to how participants experience and understand the concept, will then be used as a basis for viewing time of death through a sociological lens. Each of the four nations of the United Kingdom has their own legislative framework governing the registration and management of deaths. Unless otherwise stated, reference here is to the situation in England and Wales.

Time of Death, 59–77

Copyright © 2024 Glenys Caswell

Published under exclusive licence by Emerald Publishing Limited

doi:10.1108/978-1-80455-005-220241005

With the development of the calendar and the invention and increasing precision of clocks, greater accuracy has been possible in the recording of time of death, should this be desired (Duncan, 1999; Holford-Strevens, 2005; Richards, 1998). When someone dies in the presence of other people, perhaps family and friends or healthcare professionals, a reliable time of death may be noted, but when a death is unwitnessed, it may be much more difficult to assign a time (Black, 2018; Watson, 2011). In most circumstances, the lack of a precise time of death will not be considered as important.

The main circumstance when time of death matters is in a case of unlawful killing. The more accurately the date and time of death can be recorded, the more likely that investigators are able to pin down the alibis of people whom they may suspect of killing the deceased individual (Sachs, 2001). For this to happen, the forensic pathologist will examine the body of the deceased person in order to determine both the cause of death and the time death interval. This is not straightforward because although there are stages through which a decomposing body must go, there are many factors, both within the body and in the outside environment in which it is discovered, that affect the timing of the bodily changes (Black, 2018; Watson, 2011). The time of death is usually described, therefore, in terms of a time frame (Adam, 2004), which takes into account the different variables in the specific case. The concept of the time frame may also be useful in considering cases where technological interventions may defer death sometimes for a very short time, perhaps through a resuscitation attempt after a cardiac arrest.

In most deaths, the date of death is sufficient. After a death in the United Kingdom, there are certain procedures which must be followed. First, the death will be verified, which means that the fact of death is confirmed. This procedure may be carried out by an appropriately qualified nurse and it will be followed by the certification of death (Wilson et al., 2019). This is a legal requirement, and the certificate must be completed by a medical practitioner, prior to the registration of the death. The certificate includes cause of death and also the date on which certification takes place; if a death happens in the hours before midnight, the date on the certificate may be the day following the date on which the death occurred if there is a delay in the medical practitioner viewing the body (Office for National Statistics, 2008).

Data from death certificates and registrations are gathered by state agencies in the nations of the United Kingdom and included in national statistical data sets. Each of these agencies produces official statistics which are intended for use by government and its agencies, businesses, citizens, researchers, scholars, appropriate international organisations and students. In relation to deaths, the data include information about the numbers of people who die, where in the country they die, their age at death, when in the year they die and what they die of. Access to this information assists in the planning of services such as end of life care or the provision of cemeteries and crematoria. For such planning to meet the needs to which it is addressed, it is essential for the statistical data to be reliable, that is, for the data to be trustworthy and representative of what they purport to be (Higgs, 2004).

It will be argued here that the date of death data are not necessarily accurate, as they typically record date of certification. As noted above, the main reason for wanting an accurate and precise date and time of death is to aid homicide investigation. For most purposes, within 24 hours is reliable enough so that when a doctor certifies a death after midnight, it does not matter from a statistical point of view that the death took place the previous day. This is usual practice and is therefore considered reliable, as all are treated the same.

There is, however, a group of deaths which are different. These are deaths where someone dies alone, and their body is undiscovered for an extended period of time. When someone is found in such circumstances, unless there are indications of third-party involvement in the death, the date of death will be recorded on the death certificate as the date on which the body was found. The way in which this occurs and the possible reasons for it were considered at some length by the funeral director and the anatomical pathology technologist (APT) in study 1, and this will be reviewed here. Sometimes, a body will be found years after the death (Black, 2018; Caswell, 2022), although more commonly it will be weeks or months. How often this happens in the United Kingdom is unknown because this is not information which is routinely collected and published in the official statistics. Each death of this kind is subject to an investigation by the local coroner, given a date of death and a cause which is likely to be recorded as 'unascertained' on death certificates in England and Wales and which could translate as 'unattended death, found dead' in the World Health Organization's (WHO's) classification of causes of death (World Health Organization, 2021). The existence of such a category within the WHO classification system suggests that these deaths, while no doubt a minority of the overall number of deaths, still represent a large enough number to require counting.

This chapter reviews the procedures by which time of death is established for most deaths, where there is no concern that the death was caused by someone else, and including cases where the person died alone and their body was undiscovered for an extended period of time. It also includes the situation where a death has been deferred by the use of technology and cases where an individual is missing from their home and is presumed to be dead.

The case will be made for the bureaucratisation of the measurement of time of death, with a consequent tension between the need for an accurate date of death in certain cases and the requirement for reliable statistical data to enable society-wide planning. The question will be asked about what picture this presents of dying in the United Kingdom today and whether the state processes for the gathering of statistics represent a concern for the welfare of the populace or the desire to engage in a strategy of control. The suggestion is made that the time of death is a legal convention which is operationalised by medicine, and the chapter's conclusion lays out what is being taken forward for the main argument of the book in relation to time of death and its meaning.

As well as literature, there is empirical data included in this chapter. This is drawn from palliative care nurses relating to their experiences with people dying and the processes involved in managing the situation. Also included are data from an APT, a funeral director, and Dr Stuart Hamilton, a forensic pathologist. Case studies of people who died alone at home and whose bodies were found a long time after their death are included. This chapter begins, however, by thinking about the impetus which is behind the human wish to measure and record the time at which a person dies.

The Impetus to Record and Measure Time of Death

This section considers what it is that prompts people, both individually and collectively, to make the attempt to measure and record the time of a person's death. As was suggested in Chapter 2, societal understanding of time in the United Kingdom is as a linear progression from the past, through the present and into the future. The shared ability to measure time is critical for the functioning of a capitalist society. The majority of adults are workers who sell their labour for money in order to act as consumers and survive in a consumerist world. To be an effective worker requires the individual to turn up at an agreed time to the workplace, which may be a geographical location or an online space (Bailey & Madden, 2017).

The UK economy is dependent upon the selling of services which include such things as travel and the hospitality industries which need efficient timekeeping systems in order to work well. For example, travel into and from the United Kingdom was restricted during the height of the COVID-19 pandemic, and airlines and airports laid off members of staff. During the summer of 2022, as the numbers of people wishing to travel rose again, flights did not run to timetable and a number were cancelled with short notice to intending passengers (Topham, 2022). Reports of chaos at UK airports show the frustration felt by travellers whose flights did not run to timetable in the wake of COVID-19 pandemic cutbacks (Topham, 2022).

Time is also key to the functioning of educational institutions, where timetables schedule the work of teaching staff and the learning of pupils and students. It is also used as way of setting targets for diagnosis and treatment within the National Health Service (NHS). Government targets are set, for example, for the start of treatment for cancer once it has been diagnosed. There was a perception during the COVID-19 pandemic that targets were often not being met, leading to potentially worse outcomes for people with a cancer diagnosis (Nuffield Trust, 2022). Thus, time is part of the basis of social functioning in the United Kingdom, and it permeates all aspects of life, work and leisure, including the ways in which society manages death and dying.

In the 21st century, every death is required to be seen, both legally and by social imperative, and one of the lenses used is that of time. This has come about through a process of change over time. Historically, caring for people who were dying and ensuring their safe onward passage to the afterlife was the responsibility of families, the church and local communities. Gradually, this has changed in the United Kingdom, with increasing individualisation and reliance on outsourcing to professionals, such as healthcare workers and funeral directors (Howarth, 2007). Advances in scientific methods and increased understanding of the human body and the effects of disease have enabled physicians to become more effective in staving off early death. Changes to the medical profession began in the United

Kingdom in the 19th century, with growing numbers of universities offering medical degrees and the beginnings of the regulation of medical practitioners (Watson, 2011). The 19th century also saw a number of landmarks in medical practice, including the development of the germ theory of disease, the first successful human blood transfusion, the first use of a general anaesthetic and the development of vaccines (Hajar, 2015). Together, these developments contributed to the establishment of an environment in which it seemed desirable to begin the process of monitoring the health of the population of England and Wales.

The 1836 Registration Act established the General Register Office for England and Wales, and for the first time, the Act required that all births and deaths taking place within those 2 countries must be registered (Higgs, 2004). At various times, the 1836 Act has been updated so that, for example, since 1874, it has been necessary for a medical practitioner to sign a certificate of cause of death, with cases where there is doubt about the cause being referred to a coroner. The 1926 Act made it unlawful to dispose of a body prior to the registration of the death and also required stillborn babies to have their deaths registered (UK Parliament, 2014). It is estimated that in 2019, 96% of deaths which took place in the United Kingdom were registered (Dattani, 2023).

There have been further changes to practise in the 21st century, with the passing of the Coroners and Justice Act by the UK parliament in 2009, which was brought into force in England and Wales in July 2013. This Act forms the context within which deaths are recorded in the 2020s. When there is doubt as to the cause of a death, suspicion that the death may have been caused by a third party or the individual themselves or where there is uncertainty about the identity of the deceased person, then the death must be reported to the coroner who will institute an investigation if they deem it necessary. For deaths which do not require reporting to the coroner, the cause of death will be agreed by the doctor responsible for the care of the person who died and the medical examiner. The office of medical examiner is a new one for England and Wales and, at the time of writing, it was still in the process of being rolled out across the counties (National Medical Examiner, 2023).

One of the key reasons for gathering population level data about deaths is to try and reduce the numbers of deaths so that the population will live longer lives. Related to this, it is important to certify deaths with accurate information for a number of reasons. Such information allows the measurement of the contribution which different diseases make to the population's mortality, as well as to the monitoring of population health and the design and evaluation of public health interventions and the planning of health services. In addition, such statistics are used in a wide range of research projects on the health, morbidity and death of the populations of England and Wales (Fairbairn, 2021). The date on which the individual died was included in the earliest national registrations (Fairbairn, 2021).

The collection of official statistics is intended to be for the public good, and they are held and made publicly available for a variety of reasons. These include allowing the population to assess their government's actions and policies, providing a view of the nation and its people for legislators, enhancing the ability of the government to make informed choices when carrying out the business of government and giving international bodies the evidence needed to make cross-country comparisons. Official statistics are also intended to assist the work of analysts, researchers, scholars and students, as well as provide businesses with the data that they require to run efficiently (Allin, 2022).[1]

The WHO's template for a death certificate is readily available online, along with a guide to its use and the most up-to-date version of the *International Classification of Diseases*.[2] There is no legal requirement for member states to make use of the template, and different countries take different approaches to registering the deaths of their citizens. China, for example, has a population of approximately 1.4 billion people. People are encouraged to register deaths which occur, and it was estimated in 2018 that just under 75% of deaths were registered (Zeng et al., 2020). The population of India is second only to that of China, and it is estimated that 17% of all global deaths occur there each year. Efforts are being made to increase the registration of deaths in India, from a belief that mortality data are key to the improvement of public health. Between 2000 and 2018, the rate of registrations increased from 58% to 81%. It is notable, however, that the rate of registration of female deaths is lower than that of males, 74% compared to 85% in 2018 (Basu & Adair, 2021). In 2014, the WHO estimated that about two thirds of all deaths are unregistered each year, which is about 38 million deaths out of 56 million.[3]

Even when a death certificate is issued following someone's death, that does not necessarily mean that there is in place an accurate record of the individual's death. A literature review and analysis found that errors in completing death certificates are common globally, with 80% not including the time period between onset of final disease and death and 45% not including comorbidities or including inappropriate ones. The least common error was illegible handwriting on the certificate, which featured in about 12% of certificates (Alipour & Payandeh, 2021). Although the WHO recommends inclusion of date of death on the certificate, this was not included in the review of errors. It would, of course, be impossible for reviewers to know whether or not the date of death was correct, and so it would not be possible to include in any such evaluation of death certificates. This issue will be revisited below.

It is not only the state, however, which has an interest in when an individual dies; those who are bereaved also need to know when someone they care about has died. The knowledge that someone significant to us has died is hard to take, but it is important knowledge. Grieving may take place over an extended period

---

[1]Office for National Statistics, 'Statistics we produce', https://www.ons.gov.uk/aboutus/whatwedo/statistics/statisticsweproduce

[2]World Health Organization, 2023, Medical Certification - International form of medical certificate of cause of death, https://www.who.int/standards/classifications/classification-of-diseases/cause-of-death

[3]World Health Organization, 2014, Civil registration: why counting births and deaths is important, https://www.who.int/news-room/fact-sheets/detail/civil-registration-why-counting-births-and-deaths-is-important

of time which sometimes begins prior to the person's biological death where it is described as experiencing anticipatory grief. Such grieving has been identified, for example, in relationships where the person dying has dementia or they have been diagnosed with a terminal illness (Dehpour & Koffman, 2023; Majid & Akande, 2022).

Whenever grief may start, the knowledge that the death has occurred is important for those who are bereaved, and it is also the case that until the death is known, the required social processes cannot be put in place. The funeral is often spoken of as something that has to be endured, yet it is one of the social rites which take place after a death. The death must be registered, the funeral arranged and appropriate notices about the death must be placed so that those who need to know are informed. These processes are about engaging with the social circle which may be a source of support to the bereaved family (Woodthorpe, 2017).

The push to record when a death occurs therefore comes from both the state and the people who are bereaved by a particular death. While there are crossovers between the way in which the time of death is perceived by those who are bereaved as compared to the way in which the state records it, it is the case that individuals who are mourning a death experience and feel the time around the death in a much more personal way. This is not surprising, and this topic forms the focus of Chapter 6. This chapter remains, however, with the issue of recording time of death for statistical and legal reasons.

Recording Date and Time of a Death in Practice

Accuracy Versus Reliability

Time keeping has become more sophisticated during the 20th and 21st centuries. This seems to make it a straightforward proposition to record the date and time at which someone died and to an extent this is true in that the recording of a time in hours and minutes is not difficult. What can be problematic, however, is that it can sometimes be hard to tell precisely when someone died. For statistical purposes, it may be that reliability is sufficient, given that a dictionary definition of reliable is that 'Someone or something that is reliable can be trusted or believed because he, she, or it works or behaves well in the way you expect'.[4] The dictionary definition of accuracy, on the other hand, suggests that data are 'correct, exact, and without any mistakes'.[5] The notion of the accuracy of data therefore suggests exactitude, while reliability suggests trustworthiness.

Witnessed Dying

When a dying person is accompanied by others, it should be a simple matter to note a reasonably accurate time of death (Black, 2018). This is the case despite difficulties in defining exactly when a death occurs and the fact that sometimes

---

[4]Reliable: https://dictionary.cambridge.org/dictionary/english/reliable
[5]Accurate: https://dictionary.cambridge.org/dictionary/english/accurate

family members fail to realise that death has occurred or if the death happens when they are away from the bedside (Caswell & O'Connor, 2019; Donnelly & Battley, 2010; Donnelly & Donnelly, 2006; Kellehear, 2013; Valentine, 2007). Filmmaker Steven Eastwood released a documentary in 2018 called *The Island* in which he followed and filmed four terminally ill people over a year.[6] In the film, Eastwood sits with, and films, one of the men as he is dying. It is impossible to tell from the film the exact moment when he died (Clarke, 2018).

When someone dies an assisted death, it is to be expected that their dying will be witnessed. Such a death is illegal in all four nations of the United Kingdom, and the Campaign for Dignity in Dying, which campaigns for a change to the laws in the United Kingdom, claims that a Briton travels to Switzerland once every eight days to die at Dignitas.[7] The service offered by Dignitas in Switzerland includes the accompaniment of the dying person by at least two local people when they die. This is termed accompanied suicide, and professional watchers are required by Swiss law in addition to any family or friends who may be present.[8]

While this knowledge of when a person dies may be important to those who knew them, it does not necessarily form the basis of the official data about the when of their dying. Bureaucratic systems have their own needs and processes in place to meet those needs. Information about when individuals die is only one facet, and a small facet, of that information. The following sections address the ways in which time of death is dealt with in England and Wales.

Forensic Cases

Accuracy matters in the case of homicide, as the closer to an accurate time of death that can be established the better, so that investigators can assess suspects' alibis and work towards finding the culprit (Sachs, 2001; Sibbens et al., 2017). The attempt to pin down the date and time of death devolves on the forensic pathologist and their skill in evaluating the body of the deceased person and determining the time death interval (Black, 2018).[9] This is not straightforward because although there are seven stages of change in the body after death which can aid in establishing the time death interval, there are also factors, within the body and the outside environment in which it is discovered, that affect the timing of the bodily changes (Black, 2018; Watson, 2011).

Academic literature demonstrates an ongoing process of trying to establish ways of pinpointing the time death interval ever more accurately. Avenues pursued in this endeavour include, among other things, studying the

---

[6]The Island: https://www.islandfilm.co.uk/

[7]Campaign for Dignity in Dying, Dignitas, https://www.dignityindying.org.uk/why-we-need-change/dignitas/

[8]Dignitas, Accompanied Suicide, http://www.dignitas.ch/index.php?option=com_content&view=article&id=20&Itemid=60&lang=en

[9]The period of time which elapses between the death of the individual and the time at which the post-mortem is carried out is described by different phrases, including 'time since death' (Shrestha et al., 2021); 'post-mortem interval' (Matuszewski, 2021).

temperature-dependent post-mortem degradation of cardiac troponin-T, the use of forensic entomology, exploration of the use of circadian biomarkers as forensic molecular clock markers and the analysis of potassium levels in the vitreous fluid in the eye (Kumar et al., 2016; Madea, 2016; Matuszewski, 2021; Sibbens et al., 2017; Zilg et al., 2015).

Conversation with Dr Hamilton, the forensic pathologist quoted in Chapter 3, however, revealed that despite all the research that is being conducted, identifying the time when a person died continues to be difficult, if not impossible. He said that there is too much variability in all the different ways that are currently in use, from rigour mortis to the pooling of blood (hypostasis), to body temperature to the level of bodily decomposition. Dr Hamilton went on to say:

> So my standard answer, which I have used in court, is that somebody died between the last time they were reliably known to be alive and when they were legally declared dead and anything that I said based on factors from the body is at best unhelpful and at worst actively misleading.

Dr Hamilton also suggested that the increasing sophistication and widespread use of technology can sometimes offer an alternative route to accurate information on timings. The widespread placing of closed circuit television (CCTV), particularly in urban areas, may capture images of when an event occurs. At the individual level, data from mobile phones, smart watches and accessories, such as Fitbits which track people's physical activity, may provide clues about the timing of when the person's body ceased all activity.

So it seems that the time of death is best described in terms of a time frame, which takes into account the different variables in the specific case. These variables may include biological data but equally may comprise data from technologies external to the deceased individual (Adam, 2004). Increasing knowledge has, according to Dr Hamilton, created a situation in which pathologists feel less able to pronounce on time of death as they consider the variability to be found not only in the environment in which a body died but also within the body itself.

Non-forensic Cases

All deaths in the United Kingdom must be certified and registered before the body disposal and funeral can take place. The death certificate records only the date of death, and this is what goes into the national statistical data set. After a death in the United Kingdom, there are certain procedures which must be followed. For a person who dies under the care of health professionals, the death will first be verified, which means that the fact of death is confirmed. This may be carried out by an appropriately trained and qualified nurse, and protocol suggests it should occur within an hour in a hospital setting and within four hours in a community setting. The date and time will be noted in the deceased person's notes, and this forms the official time of death (Wilson et al., 2019).

Certification of death is a legal requirement, and the certificate must be completed by a medical practitioner, prior to the registration of the death. As noted above, the procedures in use in England and Wales are in process of change as the Coroners and Justice Act 2009 is implemented. The death certificate includes cause of death and also the date on which certification takes place. If a death happens in the hours before midnight, the date on the certificate may be the day following the date of death (Office for National Statistics, 2008).

Once a death has been certified, it is necessary to register it, prior to under-taking the funeral and disposal of the body. When the method of disposal is to be a cremation, there is an application form to be completed, which requires inclusion of the date and time of death.[10] Overall, cremation is the preferred method of disposal in the United Kingdom. In 2020, almost 81% of funerals in England and Wales were cremations; in Scotland, the cremation rate was just under 71%, but Northern Ireland is different with slightly over 22% of funerals resulting in a cremation. The provisional rate of cremations for the United Kingdom in 2020 is 78.45%.[11] In the majority of deaths, therefore, in the United Kingdom, the official time of death is required for the requisite paperwork to enable a cremation to take place.

The palliative care nurse who took part in study 1 spoke about the process of death verification. She said:

> My understanding is that it is, yes you would put the time of death. Now it seems to be an estimate, yeah because there can be a big pause in the pattern and time becomes irrelevant really. But it is completed on the form. I suppose the main thing is that if it's pre or post-midnight we have an estimate of the date itself, you know, that can happen as well.

The nurse suggests that both date and time may sometimes be inaccurate when recorded in a person's medical and nursing notes after they have died.

The funeral director, also from study 1, spoke about the process of certifying deaths and how this can sometimes be problematic for families. In her experience:

> We have had situations where families have been to the register office to register the death and the medical certificate has said a different date. But I have spoken with the register office on a number of occasions when this has happened and they have said to us that they will honour the date that the family knew that the death occurred, regardless of the fact that the certificate might not have been issued until the following day... And so really what I'm

---

[10]Ministry of Justice, UK Government, 'Cremation forms and guidance' (2022): https://www.gov.uk/government/collections/cremation-forms-and-guidance

[11]The Cremation Society, Progress of cremation in the British Islands 1885–2020, https://www.cremation.org.uk/progress-of-cremation-united-kingdom

saying is yes, the date of death, it's very important for families that that date is the date that they are aware that death occurred.

From the funeral director's perspective, as someone who worked with families at the point of registering the death and making funeral arrangements, family members sometimes expressed concern when the date on the death certificate was the day after they believed the death to have occurred. People feel that they know when the person they care about died, yet the wrong date on the certificate held the potential for them to worry that their person was not dead when they were originally told that they were, and that the professionals had made a mistake.

Data from death certificates are included in the official statistical data set managed in England and Wales by the Office for National Statistics, with much of the information publicly available.[12] In Scotland, this service is provided by the National Records of Scotland[13] and in Northern Ireland by the Northern Ireland Statistics and Research Agency.[14] In all four countries, data are population level as information on individual deaths is not made available to the public. Data on time of death are not necessarily accurate, given that certification may take place some hours after death has occurred, but they are reliable, given that the method of recording is consistent across death certificates.

Deferment of Death Through Technological Intervention

Situations exist where an individual meets the local criteria for being diagnosed as dead, except for the fact that medical technology keeps their heart beating and their lungs breathing. In such circumstances, the death has not officially occurred until such time as it is certified by a medical practitioner, which will be once the machines are switched off.

When Time of Death Cannot Be Known

Socially Proscribed Deaths

Genocides/Crimes Against Humanity

As has already been noted, genocide occurs when members of a group within a nation state are targeted and murdered, with the sanction of the state (Williams & Pfeiffer, 2017). The bodies of those who are killed in this way are not returned to families, who often are left for many years without knowing what happened. In many cases, family members die without ever knowing for sure the fate of their

---

[12]Office for National Statistics, England and Wales: https://www.ons.gov.uk/peoplepopulationandcommunity/birthsdeathsandmarriages/deaths

[13]National Records of Scotland: https://www.nrscotland.gov.uk/statistics-and-data/statistics/statistics-by-theme/vital-events/deaths

[14]Northern Ireland Statistics and Research Agency: https://www.nisra.gov.uk/statistics/births-deaths-and-marriages/deaths

person who disappeared. The uncertainty and the efforts which family members may make to try and find their person, or to discover what happened to them, can cause significant suffering, both emotional and practical (International Committee of the Red Cross, 2017).

While the likelihood is that their person is dead, the family have no way of knowing how or when the death occurred. Efforts are made by organisations such as the International Committee of the Red Cross (ICRC) to find and identify the bodies of people who have been subjected to genocidal attacks. Forensic specialists of many kinds are involved in such work and, in many cases, families are also key to the tasks of finding and identifying bodies (Black, 2018; Moon, 2019). The role of 'humanitarian forensic action' is concerned with the exhumation and identification of the bodies of people who have died in mass atrocities and returning them to their families so that they are able to carry out the rites that they feel appropriate (Moon, 2019, 2020). The clock and calendar time when their person died can never be known, and the lost time of their separation can never be regained. However, the return of their person's body brings certainty of the death and restores a modicum of control over what happens next. This reunion of families and their deceased members is a form of time restored, bringing their timelines together again.[15]

People Who Die When Alone

There is a group of deaths which are not forensic cases but neither are they straightforward deaths. These are deaths where someone dies alone, and their body is undiscovered for an extended period of time. When someone is found in such circumstances, unless there are indications of third party intervention in the death, in which case there will be a forensic examination and a police enquiry, the date of death will be recorded on the death certificate as the date on which the body was found (Caswell, 2022). This is inaccurate. Sometimes a body will be found years after the death (Black, 2018; Caswell, 2022), although more commonly it will be days, weeks or months. How often this happens in the United Kingdom is unknown because this is not information which is gathered for the statistical data set. Each death of this kind is subject to an investigation by the local coroner, but most do not categorise deaths in such a way as to make the information easy to extract. This group of people is invisible, both before and after death. However, after death, there are social processes put in train to bring them back into the statistical fold. The individuals and their deaths are examined, given a date of death and a cause which is likely to be recorded as unascertained on death certificates in England and Wales (Caswell, 2022).

The APT who took part in study 1 reflected on this occurrence and why the date of death may be recorded as it is, saying:

---

[15]More information about genocide and efforts to combat it can be found at the Wiener Holocaust Library site: https://www.theholocaustexplained.org/what-was-the-holocaust/what-was-genocide/

> The time of death will always go as when they're found dead and not look at when they actually died. So someone could come into us and clearly have been dead for a number of months. One that always comes to mind is someone who was found, I mean there's nothing stopping them from wearing a Christmas jumper in May, but it would probably indicate that they had died at Christmas. And they were in the kind of condition where that indicated that as well. But obviously, their date of death went down as the date when they were found. It seems odd to me that it happens, but also it does make sense because you can't confirm when they did die.

The APT was able to see both sides of this issue. She noted that while it may seem odd to record a date of death that is inaccurate by months or even years, an intensive exploration of their body and circumstances would be unlikely to uncover an accurate date of death.

As part of the research in study 2, 10 case studies were compiled of people who had lived and died alone at home. The length of time their bodies were undiscovered ranged from two days to seven years, and in each case, the date of death was recorded as the date on which their body was discovered. This is usual practice as was noted by the APT. More detail about the study and the cases can be found in *Dying alone* (Caswell, 2022).

Jason[16] was one of the people included in the case studies. He was a 52 year old man who lived alone and had some health problems, although not to such an extent that he would be expected to die. His younger sister was in contact with him, mainly by phone and text as he was a heavy smoker and a hoarder so that his flat was a bit of a mess and she found being around him hard. Two weeks after her last text to him, police officers visited her to say that he had been found dead in his flat. It was not clear when he had died, but he had last been seen two weeks before his body was found. Jason's death was certified as occurring on the date that his body was found. It was difficult for his sister, as she felt that she should have followed up on his non-response to her text as it was unlike him not to reply. It was also hard for her not knowing when he had died. The coroner ordered an investigation into Jason's death and a post-mortem, which found that he died of acute upper gastrointestinal haemorrhage. There were no suspicious circumstances (Case study 1, study 2).

Jason's sister said:

> And then I texted him on the Monday, and I didn't get a reply. So I think from the post-mortem report he must have died probably around that time. I can't tell for sure but yeah... So as I said I think Jason had been there for quite a while from the report... And I just feel bad that I didn't go and visit, but that's the only thing that really plays on my mind.

---

[16]The name Jason is a pseudonym.

When someone dies alone in the way that Jason did, there are bureaucratic procedures which are instituted to neutralise the effects of a socially unacceptable death, including the assignment of a date of death when there was no possibility of knowing when the biological death took place (Caswell, 2021; Caswell, 2022). The police will be involved in the investigation on behalf of the coroner, and they will invoke estimates and assumptions about when the death occurred, based on the expiry dates of food in the house, or newspapers and television listings magazines. Such estimation stays hidden in the coronial paperwork, as the post-mortem is carried out only to eliminate the possibility of third party involvement in the death, not to understand when the death occurred (Caswell, 2022).

In two of the 10 case studies, analysis suggested that the individuals had undergone social death prior to their biological deaths. It was impossible to assign a time to this process. The discovery of their bodies and the enactment of post-death practices revived notice of them but without any sense of agency on the part of the deceased person. Local authorities have a legal responsibility to take charge when there is no family to arrange a funeral, and authorities vary in their approach to the process. In both cases where social death could be identified as having occurred at an unspecified time prior to bodily death, the individual's funeral was handled by the relevant local authority (Turner & Caswell, 2022).

Missing People

Chapter 2 noted the issue of people who go missing and the ways in which their family members who have been left behind manage time (Katz & Greene, 2021). Adults leave home and break off contact with their families and previous lives all over the world. In England and Wales, there is a legal process in place which allows their family to acquire a Declaration of Presumed Death certificate from the High Court. They can then apply to the General Register Office for a Certificate of Presumed Death. Families can utilise this procedure once their person has been missing without any indication that they are alive for seven years or sooner if there is good reason to believe that they have died. The declaration of presumed death is legal proof of the missing person's status as being believed to have died, and it includes a date and time of the presumed death.[17]

Accuracy or Reliability?

For the facilitation of investigation into homicides, accuracy in identifying the time of death and thus the time death interval is key, alongside the need to clarify the cause of death. In England and Wales, a forensic pathology service is provided by the government's Home Office. This service assists coroners and police forces in the investigation of homicides and suspicious death cases. Home

---

[17]Missing People, Presumption of death in England and Wales, 2016, https://www.missing people.org.uk/get-help/help-services/practical-help/presumption-of-death/england-and-wales

Office-registered forensic pathologists are independent of the police, coroners and the Home Office.[18]

The Office for National Statistics (2022c) publishes a monthly analysis of deaths in England and Wales, based upon death registrations. For inclusion in this data set reliability is the most appropriate approach to take, as this means that all entries into the log of deaths have been assigned dates of death in the same way, even though some of those dates are inaccurate. It is useful to record when individuals die, as there are occasions when it is helpful to analyse the mortality rates for different times of year. For example, in some years, higher numbers of people die during the cold winter months or during a summer heat wave (Healy, 2003; Klinenberg, 2001). Access to data on such deaths provides a starting point for the exploration of the phenomenon and the assessment as to whether there is a need to develop interventions to reduce the death rates.

Most of the time, however, when people die is not as important, for the state, as the cause of their death. As we have seen, errors in the completion of death certificates are common internationally, carrying the potential to skew the results of research and health service planning services based upon those certificates (Alipour & Payandeh, 2021).

Bureaucratisation of Measuring Time of Death

The Registration Act of 1836 created, for the first time, a system for the collection of population level data on births, marriages and deaths in England and Wales. Similar legislation for Scotland came into force in 1854 (Cameron, 2007). After the introduction of the Registration Act, there was suspicion among some members of the public about the government's motivation in passing the Act. Some held the belief that the real reason for the collection of national level statistics was to do with the collection of tax revenue and the control and repression of the population (Higgs, 2004, p. 22).

The bureaucratisation of death at the level of the state, which began in England and Wales with the 1836 Act and continues today with the Coroner and Justice Act 2009, gives the state and its agents the right of access to information about the lives and deaths of individuals in society. This right of access includes details about causes of death and any contributory factors and the authority to regulate citizens' deaths. State agents have the right of access to '...the interior of the corpse, into its personal biography as well as its anatomy and physiology' (Prior, 1989, pp. 199–200). In England and Wales, coroners will examine the circumstances and context of deaths where there is doubt as to cause or the identity of the deceased; in 2021, 33% of deaths in England and Wales were reported to the coroner (Ministry of Justice, 2022). Coroners have the right to order a post-mortem to be conducted and an investigation to be carried out,

---

[18]UK Government, Home Office, 2021, Forensic pathology: role within the Home Office, https://www.gov.uk/guidance/forensic-pathology-role-within-the-home-office#home-office-forensic-pathology-unit

regardless of what the deceased person's family think or want. Since 2013, however, the coroner has had a duty to try and identify the family, or personal representative, of a deceased person who comes within their jurisdiction and to inform them of the investigation that is being carried out (Kirton-Darling, 2022). Medical professionals will enquire into the physical causes of all deaths and sometimes carry out a post-mortem, thus recording what caused the death. State agents effectively have the right to police the dead (Prior, 1985, p. 167).

The Office for National Statistics describes itself as:

> the UK's largest independent producer of official statistics and its recognised national statistical institute. We are responsible for collecting and publishing statistics related to the economy, population and society at national, regional and local levels. We also conduct the census in England and Wales every 10 years.[19]

The Office for National Statistics (ONS) therefore gathers the United Kingdom's official statistics not just on deaths but on a wide range of aspects of the population's lives (Office for National Statistics, 2021). Information about health and welfare, employment, education, housing, the economy and more is garnered. This activity can be read in more than one way. It can be viewed as a government ensuring that appropriate information about the country's population is gathered to allow for the planning and provision of services which are necessary to allow the country to function efficiently and for its people to live safe and contented lives. It is also possible to read the process of collecting statistics about a population as a power strategy, as one way of exercising control over them (Smart, 2002). For example, collecting data about when and how individuals die does two things. It provides information which could allow for the development of services to give care for people who are sick and dying, in the most suitable locations. The data also provide statistics which can form the basis of legislation which controls the behaviour of the population. A ban on smoking indoors in public places was introduced in 2007. A review of the evidence published in 2011 noted that the ban had reduced the level of secondary smoking and also decreased the numbers of hospital admissions for myocardial infarctions (Bauld, 2011). This could be construed as a way of improving the nation's health, but it could also be read as a means of reducing the number of hospital admissions and thus saving resources.

Time of Death as a Legal Convention

When a person dies in the care of health professionals, their death is likely to be verified by a qualified nurse. For this to happen, in England and Wales, a form must be completed in the patient notes which includes the time of the verification of death. This is a legal requirement (Wilson et al., 2019). A doctor will then complete the medical certificate of the cause of death, and again it is a legal

---

[19]Office for National Statistics, 'About us': https://www.ons.gov.uk/aboutus

requirement to document with the date of certification (Office for National Statistics, 2008). The keeping of written records is important in the NHS, which tends to have an institutional attitude that if something is not written down and documented it did not happen, or at least it cannot be shown to have happened (Maxwell, 2013).

Deaths in the United Kingdom have, legally, to be registered. The state holds two databases, one a registration database which holds textual information about individual deaths drawn from the information given at registration of the death. This is where the information comes from when someone requests a copy of a death certificate. Then there is the statistical database which holds coded data from death registrations, with the coding mostly done now by a computer programme. So deaths become part of the statistical dataset based upon when they were registered. The registration of a death should take place within five days in England, Wales and Northern Ireland and eight days in Scotland.[20]

There is potentially a week's difference between when a death occurred and when it appears in the official statistical dataset. This is unlikely to matter, for it will still be included in the correct time of year to be part of the appropriate assessment of whether there are more deaths at one time of year than at another, and they will most likely be in the correct calendar year. The fact of the date of death being wrong when the death is registered does not matter, in so far as official statistics of the state are concerned. A much bigger issue there is around cause of death and errors in assigning it (Alipour & Payandeh, 2021). The state has little interest in when someone died, unless it is a case of homicide, so there is likely to be little interest in doing more to determine the date of death with accuracy.

The way in which time of death is recorded and entered into the statistical data sets can be seen as a matter of legal convention. In most cases, the calendrical date and clock time at which a death took place is not the matter of record. The official record consists of the time of certification of death, which is usually hours but sometimes longer, after the death occurred; this is a convenience for the medical systems involved but does not necessarily make sense to family members of the person who died, as noted by the funeral director. Certification of a death is a legal requirement which must be carried out by a suitably qualified medical practitioner. The medically recorded and certificated date of death then translates into an entry in the register of deaths up to five to eight days after registration. This is a convention of the legal world which would not necessarily make sense to family members, if they knew about it. As forensic pathologist Dr Hamilton put it, "in law you are not dead til somebody who is suitably qualified says you are".

---

[20]NI Direct government services, Registering a death with the district registrar, https://www.nidirect.gov.uk/articles/registering-death-district-registrar
UK Government, Register the death, https://www.gov.uk/after-a-death

Power Relations

Measuring the time of a death is not a neutral activity. The collection of statistics about deaths in a society and the manner in which they are recorded can be read not just as a means of benefiting the population but also as a means of controlling individuals and supporting the politically desired status quo. The legislature decides on what the state requires in terms of time of death, and medicine operationalises the requirements. Individuals have little control over how time is recorded in a case where the death is of someone they care about as the state apparatus takes over in the form of health professionals, coroners, registrars, legal professionals and police officers (Prior, 1989).

Table 1 lays out the temporal constructs which have been drawn upon in this chapter during the discussion about measuring the time of death. Collectively, the constructs demonstrate that there is more to identifying the time at which a person dies than the noting of a time and date.

Conclusion

Overall, the time at which an individual death takes place is not important to the state, despite its practice of policing dead bodies. In non-forensic cases, the date of

Table 1. Temporal Constructs Used to Measure Time of Death.

Temporal Construct	Key Features
Calendar/clock time	Time as delineated on calendars and timepieces
Time frame	Period of time within which an event occurs. In relation to measuring time, most often described by reference to clocks and calendars but other descriptors may be used, such as 'before' and 'after'
Time restored	Refers to the situation where one person is lost to those who care about them and may be believed to have been killed. When the missing person is found, identified and returned to their family and friends, this is time restored, referencing the renewed chronicity of their timelines
Unobserved time	People sometimes die when alone, at a time which is not observed or witnessed
Unknowable time	There are occasions when dying in unobserved time translates into dying at an unknowable time. This is sometimes because the person's body is found too long after death to make time since death discoverable

death is likely to be important only in terms of whether it came about as a result of something which is temporally located, such as excessive heat in summer. The notion of time of death appears to be an objective fact, yet it is clear that the endeavour to place a specific time to an individual death is subject to the impact of any number of variables.

Social dependence upon time and its measurement within a linear conception make it seem impossible to do anything other than measure time of death, just as we measure and record the time of birth. The social construction of time enables us to organise our experiences, relative to each other, so that we can acknowledge there are boundaries to a life which, once it has begun, must end at some point. Our social nature as humans makes us feel that we can do nothing other than mark and acknowledge people's date and time of birth and the date and time of their death. Anniversaries are important to people who have experienced bereavement; the anniversaries of their deceased relative's birth and death will likely be observed and marked in future years. We record dates of birth and death on gravestones, and in the 21st century, we also do so in digital cemeteries and in digital obituaries.[21]

It is clear that time in relation to death is of little interest to the state, yet its record endures as part of the remembrance of people who have died on the part of individuals who knew and cared about them. This sets the scene for the following chapter, which focuses on how people who have been bereaved experience time of death.

---

[21]Digital cemeteries, such as the World Wide Cemetery, created in 1995 by Mike Kibbee: https://cemetery.org/ or the Polish Virtual Grave, created in 2007: https://virtualgrave.eu/cemetery

Digital obituaries, such as Obituaries online: https://www.obituariesonline.co.uk/funerals/obituaries or Funeral Notices: https://funeral-notices.co.uk/national/death-notices

Chapter 6

Bereaved People's Experiences of the Time of Death

Introduction

For anyone who is bereaved by a death, their experience of the time of death is more complex and nuanced than can be described by a calendar date and a clock time. This chapter draws on interviews with people who have been bereaved and palliative care nurses to discuss experiences of time in relation to death. These discussions will then form the basis for arguing that the concept 'time of death' is socially constructed.

Study 1 focused on exploring what participants understood by the concept 'time of death'. Bereaved participants were asked to reflect on how they experienced time during the period when their person was dying and died. Interview questions were asked in an open manner which gave respondents the opportunity to interpret the topic as they wished. All participants situated the time when their person died within the longer narrative of their life, illness and dying trajectory. Most did not speak of the time of death in terms of something measurable, although a couple did offer dates and times accessed from memory or, in one case, from a diary account the participant had kept. The death referred to was, in all cases, the biological death of the body. However, some participants did talk about the ways in which they were keeping the connection with their deceased person going, in ways consonant with continuing bonds theory (Klass & Steffen, 2018).

Research participants talked time talk. Most stated that they had not thought about the experience in terms of time before, but their talk was then full of time relevant words. Of course, within the setting of an online or telephone interview, they only had words with which to convey their experiences and perspectives. Time talk is a deeply embedded part of how humans communicate, and when telling stories, there is often a chronological element. There were many crossovers in the experiences that participants described and discussed, although there were

Time of Death, 79–98
Copyright © 2024 Glenys Caswell
Published under exclusive licence by Emerald Publishing Limited
doi:10.1108/978-1-80455-005-220241006

also many differences. The term family will be used here to indicate not just those who are blood relations but all those who are emotionally close to the person who died, whether by birth, kin or friendship. Most of the deaths which participants spoke about were expected, in the sense that the person who died had been diagnosed with a terminal illness. However, this did not mean that family members knew when the death would occur, for predicting when an individual will die is difficult for clinicians to do accurately when death is not imminent (White et al., 2016).

It may seem that a bereavement involves the emotion only of the individual person and those most closely connected with them. This certainly seems resonant with the idea of a society which is highly individualised and dependent upon the actions of disparate individuals who are required to create and recreate their own identities (Bauman, 2005; Giddens, 1990, 1991). However, the apparently private trouble of a bereavement in reality transcends the private sphere and is part of the issue of bereavement on a much wider, public, scale. It has '...to do with the organization of many such milieux into the institutions of an historical society as a whole, with the ways in which various milieux overlap and interpenetrate to form the larger structure of social and historical life' (Mills, 1959, p. 8). Death and bereavement affect all members of a society at some time, thus having an effect on society as a whole which, in turn, educates individuals as to how they should manage death and bereavement.

This chapter makes the case for the social construction of time of death, using research data to illustrate and support the argument. It begins by presenting a short case study based upon interviews with four members of one family, one of whose members had died. This case study illustrates the complexity involved in trying to identify a specific time of death from the perspective of bereaved individuals. It then moves on to suggest that people who are bereaved are existing in a liminal time and space during the period when their person is dying and has died. Data will then be presented, utilising four theoretical concepts which are time-scapes, the expanded present, fluid time and ongoing relationship with the deceased person. The case for the social construction of time of death will then be offered. First, however, Table 2 presents some basic information about the research participants, their relationship with the person who died and the nature of the death. All names used are pseudonyms.

Case Study: The Death of Melanie Baker

Melanie Baker was a woman in her 30s when she developed the lung cancer which killed her. She had a husband and young daughter, parents, a brother, a nephew and two nieces, as well as many friends and work colleagues in her community development work role. Her parents, her brother and her nephew took part in separate research interviews to talk about time in relation to Melanie's death. Her

Table 2. Bereaved Participants in Study 1.

Name	Relationship of Deceased to Bereaved	Expected or Unexpected Death	Place of Death	Participant Present at Death
Jenny Fisher	Husband	Expected	Nursing home	Yes
Debbie Grant	Friend	Expected	Home	No
Mary Blythe	Husband	Expected	Home	Yes
	Mother	Expected	Home	Yes
Oscar Sims	Wife	Unexpected	Hospital A&E	No
Katie Archer	Husband	Expected	Hospital	Yes
Daisy Evans	Husband	Expected	Hospital	Yes
Bob Carstairs	Father	Expected	Hospital	No, but believed he knew when it occurred
John Baker	Daughter	Expected	Hospital	Unsure
Jane Baker	Daughter	Expected	Hospital	Yes
Paul Baker	Sister	Expected	Hospital	No
Adam Baker	Aunt	Expected	Hospital	No
Elaine White	Father	Expected	Home	Yes
	Mother	Expected	Home	Yes
Graham Munro	Wife	Unexpected	Home	No
Richard Hayden	Wife	Expected	Home	Asleep in same room
Alison Taylor	Daughter	Expected	Hospice	Yes
Alice Numan	Husband	Expected	Home	Yes
Barbara Davis	Husband	Expected	Home	No
	Son	Unexpected	Hospital	No
	Brother	Expected	Care home	No

parents, Jane and John, were present on the day she died as was her brother Paul. Her nephew, Adam, was not. Melanie had been admitted to hospital overnight, and the following day her husband had phoned his wife's parents and brother and suggested they needed to come to the hospital soon if they wished to see Melanie.

Paul, Jane and John arrived at the hospital where they found Melanie with her husband and daughter by her side plus a very close friend. By this stage, Melanie was receiving palliative care. Paul said:

So we realised that palliative meant, what that meant, that she was dying. But again we didn't think it was going to perhaps happen so quickly. She got hooked up on the palliative drugs and asked us all to leave. To go for lunch, she didn't say leave, she just said, you know, isn't it time for you all to go and have some lunch in the café. And she had a close friend there and the close friend sort of took over from the family.

Paul, his parents, brother-in-law and niece left and went to the hospital café for lunch as Melanie had suggested. They were getting ready to return to the ward when Paul received a phone call from Melanie's friend asking them to come back straight away. Paul said:

We ran back and Melanie was, well I think she was still alive when...her husband and daughter got there, they were quicker than myself and my parents but by the time we got there she'd died.

Melanie's father John was uncertain as to whether Melanie was still alive when they arrived back at her bedside. He said:

...the rapidity of her death did take us by surprise. Two hours earlier we had arrived, she was so with it, so much articulate... you know, there was no kind of dramatic last moments, sharing the moment of her passing with us, but we like to feel we were there. But I find it difficult to answer your question more openly than that.

Jane, however, confidently expressed the view that she was with her daughter as Melanie died. She said:

But we were with Melanie when she died because when I kissed her she was still warm. She looked very peaceful, in fact quite beautiful really. That was a surprise. But she looked quite beautiful and peaceful and I did give her a kiss. Oh and I talked to her. And she did move her head towards me.

The family members were interviewed separately for the research project, although they had discussed the day that Melanie died between themselves and knew each other's perspectives. Paul believed that his sister had already died by the time they returned to her bedside; John was uncertain about this but wished to support his wife, who was confident that she was with Melanie when she died and that her daughter was aware of her presence. Had an experienced health professional been present they would, perhaps, have been able to take an objective view and inform the family whether or not Melanie was alive. However, the family narratives highlight the complexity involved in trying to assign a time to death, as well as suggesting the individuality of the narratives which people hold about their experience. This will be discussed further below and in the following chapter.

Being in a Liminal Space

The bereaved participants who took part in study 1 were in a liminal time and space, outside their ordinary everyday lives. Liminal time is a concept which applies to all the experiences which bereaved research participants talked about in relation to the time of death. An individual who is in a liminal space is someone who is in the process of moving from one status to another but is, at the point of observation, in neither. Such individuals are, in effect, 'betwixt and between', as Turner expresses it (Turner, 1969, p. 95). Participants were in a time which represented a space or lacuna between when their person was still an active, embodied presence in their lives, and the time when they would be bereaved and continuing life without the embodied presence of their person.

It would be easy to assume that this change of status, from non-bereaved person to bereaved person, happens in a moment. At one level, perhaps, this is the case, for as soon as their person dies, they become a widow or widower, an orphan, a bereaved parent, sibling or friend. Integration into their new status as bereaved person, however, takes longer and is an ongoing process. And during this process, they are in a liminal time, between the time when they had not yet endured the death of their person and the time when they must learn to live without their person as an embodied presence in their daily lives.

The differing ways in which bereaved participants experienced time around the death of their person were all elements of their being in a liminal time. The timescape, whereby participants placed their experience within its temporal context; the expanded present within which the moment of death occurred; the fluidity of time across the timescape and within the expanded present; all these aspects of temporal experience place the participants in a liminal temporal space. Participants were experiencing a transition from their old life to their new one, and the difficulties involved in making this move were represented in their experiences of time.

Timescapes of Dying

Time is an integral part of human experience, yet a rarely considered one. Adam's work (2004) on timescapes demonstrates that the temporal context within which something happens is a key component of that event. A timescape is a 'cluster of temporal features' which collectively make up the temporal experience of an event (Adam, 2004, p. 143). The contribution which time makes to any experience is greater than the noting of the time and date at which the event occurred. For example, it is necessary to consider aspects such as the duration of an event, the tempo or pace at which an activity occurs, the time frame within which it takes place and potentially many other temporal aspects in order to acquire a fully rounded picture of the occurrence (Adam, 2004, p. 144).

The biological dying of a human being is a process which takes place over a period of time which may be of varied duration, and at the end of that period a person's body is no longer alive. However, even when the body has died and is lifeless, the people who are emotionally close to that individual are not able immediately to think of the body as a corpse, as a non-human. For them, the body still holds personhood and is still considered as having the identity of the person who has died (Mathijssen, 2021). So, time of death for bereaved family members is not just about the time at which the person died as represented by calendar and clock time. It is also about the temporality of the dying process and the knowledge which those involved have of its irreversibility; there is no returning from death. In addition, the time extensions to be found in the duration, continuity and length of time the process of dying endures are important to the experience, as are the time point, the moment, instant, the now of their experience, of the death (Adam, 2004, p. 143). The manner in which family members experience the dying of their person also impacts their future lives, as they grapple with their loss.

Context matters in the telling of any story, and this is certainly the case in the stories which bereaved research participants told about the death of the person they cared about. When asked about the time when their person died, most participants said that they had not really thought about the experience in terms of time, but when they then spoke about what happened, their talk was permeated with time talk. They also told their stories in context, as one which had a beginning and a middle but, at the time of interview, no end. For an uninvolved observer, one might think of the moment of dying as the end, but for those who were bereaved, the death was far from being the end. For the people who had been bereaved, their story continued and, in that continuation, lay their grief and mourning, endured through time.

So that the account of the death made sense, bereaved participants began their stories before the point of death, perhaps when the person became ill or at the point when they realised how serious the illness was. And, as is the way with the telling of our personal stories, while there tended to be an overall narrative arc from the past, through the present and into the future, it was also the case that participants would move seamlessly between the tenses. Participants thus set their stories into context, so that they were comprehensible, and time was a key part of that context. It would make no sense, for example, to say that an individual died and then became ill, or that the funeral took place and then the person was diagnosed with a terminal illness. They told their stories secure in the knowledge that although they may not have thought about the temporal elements of their experience, those temporal elements were safe and fixed so that their listener would understand the temporal elements and would use them to make sense of what they were saying. I, as the listener, would know the temporal order of events, even without knowing the specific nature of those events.

It is important to ask, however, whether those events really are fixed in time, like a fly in amber. They are not, but this is not because time itself shifts, although it may, but because in our telling of our stories, we inevitably shift events. Remembering is an act of reconstruction, as we do not have access to films or recordings of events in our brains. Thus memories are open to influence and are malleable, so that our memory shifts and we adapt our understanding and thus our recall of events. This is not lying, nor is it an attempt to deceive, but it is part of the process of trying to make sense of occurrences in our lives that are incomprehensible and of presenting them in a narrative form (Shpancer, 2020). And the temporal aspects of the story shift along with all the other elements and the ways we feel about them. This is inevitable because time is an integral part of the experience.

In telling the story of their person's dying and death, bereaved participants filled in the context of the experience, as they saw it and believed that I wanted to hear it. The context included the timescape of that experience, despite their claims to have given no prior consideration to the temporal aspects of that experience. This was not disingenuousness on the part of participants, rather it was a demonstration of the embedded nature of human understandings and experiences in relation to time. They followed tried and tested patterns of storytelling, in that their accounts were chronological. They were also interweaved with interpretation and emotional responses.

The temporal context differed between stories, of course, but there was a noticeable divergence between accounts of sudden deaths and deaths where it was known that the person was dying, even though participants may not have been aware how close to dying their person was. For example, Barbara Davis's younger son had a congenital heart defect from birth, which had required him to undergo extensive medical treatment and a number of operations. His death, however, was sudden and unexpected, taking place while he was in hospital. Barbara said:

> In fact we agreed that there wasn't much more to do because he'd had a lot of treatments and he was running on a pacemaker. One knew his condition was very serious, but he'd been like that for a bit and he was slated, the date for him to come home was up on the ward wall and that was fine and then he just deteriorated and died. And I never saw it coming. And that was a terrible shock. And I think that's made it, partly of course, in real terms it's still recent. But that's very hard to come to terms with, very hard.

Although her son's death was sudden and shocking, Barbara described its occurrence in the context of his ongoing health problems, the treatment he had been receiving and his anticipated discharge to home from hospital. For Barbara to present a coherent narrative about her son's death, it was necessary for her to place it within a context which began when he was a young child before she was even aware that he had a heart condition. She laid out, that is, the timescape within which his death took place.

Mary Blythe's experience was different from that of Barbara. She knew that her husband was dying from oesophageal cancer. He had had a number of hospital admissions, and he was discharged home to die, with Mary providing most of the care that he needed. She said of the process of him dying:

> I mean it was only a short time. It seemed to stand still a bit. It's a really, it's hard to explain it, you sort of go - it's almost as if you're in a state of numbness. So the passage of time in a way doesn't register with you... So I felt quite normal...It was as if day and night almost mingled in a little bit... So yeah, it just sort of became, it was peaceful. It was definitely peaceful. I think just a time to reflect really. And you sort of knew, you knew time was getting closer, had that definite feeling that the end was approaching.

Mary also laid out the temporal context of her experience, including some of the ways in which she experienced the passage of time. She continued working until her husband came home for the final time from hospital, at which point she took leave to care for him. Her telling of the story began when her husband experienced symptoms which led him to seek medical help and progressed through treatment attempts and the gradual realisation that his illness was terminal.

The death of Richard Hayden's wife was also anticipated, as she had motor neurone disease, and it was clear to him that she was approaching the end of her life even though he did not realise quite how close she was to dying. Richard said:

> I mean to be honest with you I didn't know she was going to die on the day she died, it was a bit of a strange ending, but I'm sure they're all strange endings. I didn't know how close she was to death, but I knew she'd more or less stopped eating. So I mean she wanted to go, there's no two ways about it. Because she'd lost all her dignity, and she'd almost lost the use of her arms, and she was stuck in bed at that point in the last few days... For somebody that way, so she'd expressed a desire that she wanted to go now, she'd had enough, because basically she couldn't eat, she couldn't swallow, her voice was going. So everything was declining, but I didn't know no, she was that close to it. I mean perhaps on reflection maybe I should have done, or maybe I should have asked the question, but I didn't, I just kept plodding on, are you with me?

The way in which Richard described his wife's death included the period from when she had first experienced symptoms and been diagnosed as having motor neurone disease, through the time as her symptoms worsened and it became more difficult for her to maintain a degree of independence. Eventually, she became bed bound and, as her muscles weakened and the disease began to affect her ability to eat, she indicated that she wished her life to end and Richard realised that she would not live for much longer.

As these extracts illustrate, Barbara, Mary and Richard, in their different ways, presented the timescape within which they experienced the death of their person. All participants offered a chronologically informed narrative which drew on concepts such as duration, pace, timing, synchronisation, time sequences and patterns in order to make sense of their experience. Their stories did not end with the death of their person, as the impact of time did not end with the biological death. Participants largely offered this temporal context without reference to measured and recorded time. A loose relationship with timepieces and calendars was a consistent factor in participants' accounts.

The Expanded Present

The moment of the death took place within the expanded present. Time as it is understood and measured in normal circumstances still existed and some participants were aware of it, but the way in which it moved appeared different to them. Some participants were not at all aware of time, while others felt its difference; effectively they were outside the normal time parameters. Time was suspended in an expanded present as the person about whom participants cared was dying and died (Baraitser, 2017). The moment of dying is important, and most bereaved people wished to be with their dying person at that moment and to be aware of it. However, it was a moment which was within and subsumed by an expanded present. This encompassed the period when their person was dying, the time point at which they died and the immediate aftermath, before the future began without the embodied presence of their now deceased person.

The date of death was held in memory by participants, but otherwise dates and times were less impactful than might be expected. Katie Archer, for example, said 'my memory is very poor', and she opened her diary and read off the dates from that detailing when her husband had been diagnosed with testicular cancer and then admitted to the hospital where he died. Mary Blythe recalled that her husband '. . .died on the 10th of January. I think the funeral was, I can't remember, about the 21st, about 11 days later'.

Jenny Fisher's husband had a brain tumour which was diagnosed about 11 months before his death, and he died in a nursing home to which he had been admitted for the last three weeks of his life. She said of his death:

> So I'd discussed that with the staff at the nursing home and I had a
> call fairly early in the morning, half six-ish something like that and
> they were like you need to come in now, it's not going to be much
> longer. And they were really open about that really. So yeah I went
> in and I was there with him for the last few hours of his life,

yeah... his breathing was getting more difficult and he stopped breathing and then he would go and start again. So yeah I was aware. He was quite noisy, not noisy, it's not the right word, but the deep breath in and it would start again and then it would stop again and then just kind of went and that's really stopped now... But from my perspective now it feels like it went quite quickly. But whether it did at the time I don't remember being conscious of it either going quickly or slowly at the time. But my sense of it now is that it went quite quickly those last few days. I think probably just because I was numb...So then when he did die and I pushed the buzzer it felt like it took forever for somebody to come. That felt long. It probably wasn't, but I was just like come on, I've got to tell someone. Very odd, very strange how that sense of time differs at different points really.

Jenny was aware that her husband was dying. She wished to be with him when he died, and so paid attention to his breathing although the way in which his breathing appeared to stop before starting again, made it difficult for her to be sure when his death had occurred. Her sense of time was not operating normally and, in retrospect, she felt that time had probably gone quickly, although once she tried to summon assistance after her husband died, it slowed right down. Although Jenny's husband (probably) died when his breathing appeared to have stopped, the time of death for Jenny was a moment within the expanded present. She needed to tell someone else of her husband's death in order for it to become a reality.

Elaine White and her sister stayed with their mother when she was approaching the end of her life. Elaine found this a very difficult time, saying:

She (my mother) started sleeping for incredibly long periods of time, and just becoming weaker and really frail. And I suppose, my sister and I, it was quite obvious that she was going to die at some stage and I think we thought she would just maybe die in her sleep or just sort of fade away, but actually what happened was totally different. She had another one of these brain haemorrhages in the night and she died 11 days later. And she stayed at home, and it was those 11 days which were utterly traumatic, and they weren't at all what we were expecting... And then after 11 days she died.

For Elaine, the traumatic nature of the final 11 days of her mother's life and the way in which she died effectively drowned out the time of her mother's death. Elaine was left with a strong memory of an expanded present during which her mother, her sister and she herself endured and waited for the end of her mother's life. A traumatic time, the memory of which stayed with Elaine.

The Time of Death

So, was there an identifiable time of death for participants? The date on which the death occurred was memorable in some cases, such as for Paul Baker and his family, because his sister died on her own daughter's birthday, making the day significant at the time and in the future. Other anniversaries also took on significance, however, particularly the birthday of the person who had died. Elaine White, for example, said 'I don't think they're (anniversaries) difficult but I mean certainly we always remember her (my mother's) birthday and my father's birthday and a lot of things remind me of my mother'.

The time of day at which their person died appeared to have been less important to participants. They all wished to be with their person as they died, but this was not always possible.

Being Present at the Moment of Death

Alice Numan was present when her husband died. She said:

> my husband died of cancer. He died on the 29th of September, two years after being diagnosed with advanced cancer and just before his birthday. And I was present at his moment of dying... just told him, basically told him he'd done what he needed to do. He'd done a lot of things and I told him that he could go. And he did opt to go at that point.

This was an important moment for Alice. She had ensured that over the last hours of his life, her husband had been continuously accompanied, but it had been her wish that she should be with him as he died. She was aware when he died, but did not note the exact time and did not rush to call in the professionals to verify and certify that death had occurred. She felt at that point that there was no need to rush, and she wanted to give her sons time to sit with their father if they wished to do so, before the professionals took over the guardianship of her husband's body.

Alison Taylor was also present with her daughter when she died. Alison's daughter had not been married long when she was diagnosed as suffering with a brain tumour. She was in her early 30s at the time and Alison felt that she had to share the last days and hours of her daughter's life with her new husband. Alison said:

> And she died in my arms, can't ask for more than that... I had promised her that we would be with her all the way and, you know, we stuck with that. We stuck with that. And that was really really important to me.

Alison was an experienced nurse and had known that her daughter was very close to dying. Despite this knowledge, Alison experienced her daughter's death as a mother, not a health professional, and she stayed with her daughter for some time after she had died in the expanded present which she experienced.

Missing the Moment of Death

Some participants were not present when their person died. This is a familiar phenomenon in the world of palliative care, in which family members may spend a long time sitting with and keeping vigil beside their dying person who then dies when they leave the bedside for a short time (Caswell & O'Connor, 2019).

The palliative care nurse who took part in study 1 described this phenomenon, saying:

> I think there's a mystery to certain things as well. I suppose from what I've seen and just the timing of it and in the context of the vigil and somebody being there constantly, you know, a daughter, a husband or a wife and literally they're holding hands. They may go to go to the toilet or to just, they're encouraged to have a drink or maybe step out to engage with neighbours. . .and the person may slip away or die at that time. I think there's an element of that as well, if you're holding onto me it's really hard to die, to leave, there's an attachment.

This moment, the point at which a person dies, remains something of a mystery despite all the research and scholarship invested in trying to understand it. Some professionals, like the palliative care nurse quoted above, believe that the dying person has a degree of choice or control at this point.

Bob Carstairs was not present when his father died. This had taken place almost 50 years before the time of the interview, yet Bob recalled it vividly and became emotional speaking about it. Bob said of the moment when his father died:

> But anyway on the Friday I went and fetched his brothers to see him and, I believe, this is only my belief, I'm not asking anybody else to believe me, but because he was in so much pain I always say that he passed at three o'clock when I travelled over the (name) Bridge – because I looked up into the sky, blue sky, bright blue sky and that's how he passed on because of the pain.

Bob felt that he knew the moment when his father died and, certainly, by the time he reached the hospital his father was dead.

Oscar Sims was not with his wife when she died. She had collapsed suddenly at home and Oscar had called an ambulance. He went with her to the hospital, but she died while medical staff continued the work of the paramedics to try and save her life. Oscar said:

> So we went to (the hospital) and went into the kind of waiting room. The doctor came through and said sorry there was nothing more we could do...So there was no chance to say goodbye or anything like that.

Her collapse had been unexpected as Oscar's wife had appeared to be well at the time. He was shocked and was given the opportunity to see his wife's body, but at that point the lifesaving efforts that had been made were still obvious through the presence of medical equipment. This distressed Oscar, who said 'I think it would have been better if her mouth was closed and there wasn't a tube sticking out because it looked gruesome, I suppose'. The legal realities of the situation were not apparent or important to Oscar at that point. He was shocked by his wife's collapse and death, unaware that her death would be referred to the coroner and that it would result in a post-mortem and inquiry.

Richard Hayden missed the moment when his wife died because he was asleep. He had been caring for her at home with little support. It was Richard's own choice to take on his wife's care; he knew that her time was limited and he wanted to share as much of it as possible with her. However, it did mean that he became exhausted, so that he slept through the night which was unusual. Richard said:

> And then when, I was absolutely spent to be honest with you at that time, because I'd been non-stop awake for a few days. And I gave myself, not morphine but I dosed myself up with aspirins and paracetamols and stuff, and I thought I must sleep, I'm dead. And I did go to sleep, and I woke up in the morning circa eight o'clock, and the phone rang and it was the district nurse again... I got out of bed, it's in the same room, and I'd got all my clothes ready and I didn't even put the lights on, put my clothes on in the dark, because I didn't want to disturb (my wife) you see. And I walked over to her and I was worried. I think she was breathing, to this day I don't know, I think she was, but definitely everything was slowing down, are you with me?... I said (to the district nurse) I'm slightly worried about her, I said she's not right, I think she's all right but I'm not sure. So I took the, I might get a bit here, I took the phone through and touched her, because I hadn't touched her before, and she was cold... So I feel guilty about that, I feel guilty that I wasn't with her holding her hand and stuff like that.

Because he was asleep when she was dying, Richard expressed feelings of guilt. This is not unusual in family members who are not present when their person dies.

Witnessed/Unwitnessed Dying

The existence of an objective moment of death which can be witnessed depends upon a dichotomous view in which a person is either dead or alive at any specific moment. For people who care about the dying person and who are present when they are dying, witnessing the moment of death depends, perhaps, upon the relationships involved and how they perceive and construct what is happening (Kastenbaum, 1999). The experiences and beliefs of the Baker family, for example, demonstrate how people can have different perceptions of when the moment of death occurs. This makes the noting of a recordable time of death tricky.

Fluid Time

Zygmunt Bauman posits that we are living in a time of constant changes, and that we experience multiple endings and beginnings, so much so that we have very little time in which to establish routines and habits before everything changes again (Bauman, 2005, 2006). He further suggests, as have others before and after him and as discussed in Chapter 3, that humans are afraid of death; they know that they will die and this knowledge prompts a range of behaviours designed either to manage the fear or defer dying. One of these behaviours is that of striving for immortality. For some, this is through a belief in the reality of eternal life as offered by a religious faith, but for others, it is through forging a legacy which will survive them and cause them to be remembered (Bauman, 1992). For the bereaved research participants who took part in study 1, time was experienced as fluid, in that it was subject to change. It continued to flow, although sometimes it appeared to come to a halt; it would speed up and slow down; time became unpredictable during the period when they waited for their person to die, and it continued to be so after the death.

Jenny Fisher spoke about how her husband:

> changed so much in that relatively short period of time, 10–11 months, it feels now like it was really stretched out. But also I feel it didn't happen very slowly. It's really difficult to describe, it's a bit of both really. And it was in phases as well for him; it wasn't an all at once kind of a thing. But it kind of feels stretched out. But also it's not a lot of time we had together. Yeah it's bizarre to try and describe those differing senses of it really. Very odd when I look back, yeah. I'd not really considered that. I quite often think about how it feels like a long time since I've seen him and I often think well it's, and then I look at his photo and it feels like it's no time at all as well. So it's those two things at the same time.

Jenny struggled to make sense of how time behaved, during the period when her husband was dying and also after his death. Her sense was that time was also erratic for him, in that it was simultaneously stretched out and short for them both.

Alice Numan also experienced the passage of time as somewhat fluid, during the period of her husband's dying and after his death:

> the time with him was all skewed... A settled overall view and memory of my whole time of knowing him was really disrupted because it was just, the last few years it was just very much that massive huge experience and the fact it changed us. And then of course after the death, like most people, most of my memories were those quite traumatic ones...So that has changed and it's taken time...And then I think time did both compress and lengthen at the end.

In similar fashion to Jenny, for whom time was long and short, for Alice it was compressed and lengthened. Alice felt, further, that the period of her husband's dying disrupted the entire duration of their relationship. This came about because his becoming terminally ill when they had two school-aged children and they were both forging successful careers was such a 'massive huge experience' which changed them as individuals and within the context of their relationship.

After Alison Taylor's daughter died, she took the birth congratulations cards that she had received when her daughter was born to the funeral home and asked the funeral director to put them in the coffin, 'Because I felt that, you know, it's the beginning and the end, and they should be together'.

Mary Blythe found it difficult to recall time after her husband's death. She said:

> And like I say I did really do everything but it's only afterwards you look back and think gosh I can't remember, certainly the first few months after he died I really can't remember much about it. I don't remember the funeral very much, you know. I remember that I organised it all and everything went smoothly and things like that but the detail of the day I don't really. It's just a bit of a trance really.

Participants experienced the fluidity of time before, during and after the death of their person. Between them, participants experienced how time stretched and shrank, how its passage became difficult to recall, how beginnings and endings are closely linked.

Ongoing Relationships

Bereaved participants were all speaking about the biological death of their person, and at that time, none of their deceased were socially dead for them. Their person still existed for them and had not disappeared along with their body. As noted in

Chapter 3, continuing bonds bereavement theory suggests that it is not unusual to engage in an ongoing relationship with someone who has died (Klass & Steffen, 2018). Although the research focus in study 1 was on experiences around the time of death, participants did allude to experiences after the death. They might talk to, or about, their deceased person or use anniversaries to carry out certain important actions. For example, Alice Numan and her sons scattered her husband's ashes on Father's Day at a site which was of importance to the dead man.

Katie Archer spoke about how her plans for her husband's ashes had been put on hold by the COVID-19 pandemic travel restrictions. He had wanted his ashes to be scattered on Durban Beach in South Africa, but instead of that happening she still had them in a box in the cupboard under the stairs. However, Katie was not troubled by this because she knew that eventually her husband's wish would be fulfilled, and his ashes, as a physical artefact of her husband's existence, held little meaning for her. As she said, 'Robert is there in my heart not in actual things'.

Alison Taylor's daughter Rachel died when she was in her 30s. Alison maintained a long-term ongoing relationship with Rachel, but she also went to great lengths to ensure that Rachel herself had a degree of agency even after she had undergone bodily death. Rachel had been a teacher who had become ill soon after marrying and returning from honeymoon. Her illness had been short and she had died in a hospice with her mother and husband beside her. Alison was convinced that Rachel would have had a successful career in education, and described her daughter as an excellent teacher who was committed to improving the lives of children and assisting them to reach their potential.

Rachel had died about six years before Alison took part in the research, and in that time Alison had travelled abroad a few times. Whenever she travelled, Alison took with her something of Rachel's to leave in a local community which could make a difference and help improve lives. Alison had taken pencils and notebooks to schools, money to fund freshwater schemes and books.

Alison said:

> When I go abroad which I have done since she died I always...have something of hers that I can take with me to leave so that Rachel is all over the world. So she's travelled, you know, her legacy is all over the world... So all the things that I wanted and needed to do to make, to give me comfort, if you like, and to take little bits of her so that her life had influenced and benefited someone over there. That was really important to me... So she's in Africa and she's in Cambodia and, you know, she'll maybe be somewhere else as well. And that means a lot to me.

Alison was concerned with her daughter's legacy and had a strong desire to see something beneficial to others coming after her death. Alison believed that Rachel would have made a positive contribution to the world, so she therefore decided that when she travelled abroad she would take with her small things which could support children in their education, and she would do this in honour of her daughter. Alison's actions were based in the idea of her future daughter who was no longer in a position to establish her own legacy, but on whose behalf Alison could act. For Alison and her daughter, the past, present and the future were no longer operating in a linear sequence. Time was fluid, and in this fluidity, Alison was conferring a degree of social agency on her daughter. Alison knew that her daughter was dead, but simultaneously Rachel had social life.

The Social Construction of Time of Death

Bereaved participants were all well socialised into the processes of time in their social setting. They all knew how time worked, they understood the use of time pieces and calendars, they knew the importance of schedules and timetables, they understood when punctuality was, and was not, important. Their understanding and knowledge of time use in their society was so deeply embedded in them that they could function on a temporal level without even thinking about it. Time was an unconsidered yet ubiquitous aspect of their lives. Adam (1990) found when beginning her studies of the social understandings and experiences of time that people might think that it is a pointless field of study because time is 'an obvious fact of life' (Adam, 1990, p. 1).

Bereaved research participants in study 1 took time for granted in similar fashion to the way that we all do most of the time. They knew that time runs in linear fashion and that it always runs at the same speed, although this did not prevent them having experience of time appearing to behave differently. They had all had experiences where time flew, or dragged, or even appeared to stop, but they also knew that this was an illusion because time continued, their clocks and watches showed them this, while what was happening to them made it seem as if time was altered (Ogden et al., 2022).

As they were experienced social users of time, bereaved participants were adept at describing their temporal experiences, despite not having considered their experience of death and bereavement previously through a temporal lens. The ways in which participants talked of their temporal experiences at the time when their person was dying and died thus drew on previous temporal experiences. Shared understandings and the taken for granted nature of time in quotidian life, including the way in which it can seem to behave differently even when they know that it does not, gave them the necessary temporal knowledge and skills (Adam, 1990; Ogden et al., 2022).

However, the death of someone close to them is different in that it is not a daily event, and their experience of someone close to them dying was not necessarily underpinned by previous direct experience. During a lifetime, we will all experience the deaths of people around us, and how keenly we feel the bereavement depends on various factors, including how important a member of our network they were. But even those of us who have extensive social networks do not deal with death on a personal level all the time, and each experience can be different.

Participants talked about their experience of the time when their person was dying and died in a very specific sense, relating it directly to that one occasion.

Mary Blythe, for example, talked about the time when her husband and then her mother were dying. She was involved in looking after each of them as they were dying, but they were very different experiences and she, therefore, described them in terms which reflected that difference.

Bereaved participants felt each bereavement afresh and did not necessarily know what to expect when their person was dying and had died. However, they did have resources to draw on which could assist them in knowing what they should do. There are a number of cultural scripts in the United Kingdom which can act as an aid in deciding how to behave with regard to dying and death (Seale, 1998). There is a strong cultural script, for example, which informs people that they should accompany a member of their family who is dying. This script is to be found in a range of resources and is often also promoted by healthcare workers who are looking after dying people (Caswell, 2020; Caswell et al., 2022).

There is also in place a well-developed death management system run by institutions such as the legal and medical professions, organisations such as the institutional church and businesses such as funeral directors which offer expert assistance to those who require it. The assistance which professionals employed in the various sectors offer ranges from the provision of hands-on care, through giving information, advice and support as well as offering guidance on death-related social norms (Caswell, 2020; Caswell, 2022). Research participants each underwent an individual experience and they felt it as such. However, it was also informed by the social mores and norms of the social setting in which they lived.

There is no one moment which can be framed as a, or the, time of death for the bereaved participants. For them, the biological death was part of a process of bereavement, and their person continued to hold personhood for some time after the death of their body. The bereaved research participants were in a liminal emotional and temporal space when their person died, and for some this could extend over a long period of time. Alison Taylor, for example, remained in such a space more than six years after the death of her daughter. Alison not only retained an ongoing relationship with her daughter but also went to great lengths to give her daughter an extended social life after her biological death.

Time, as understood and experienced by humans in social settings, is a social construction. Human time has no demonstrable objective existence, but has been produced and reproduced over generations (Bardon, 2013; Berger & Luckmann, 1967; Bluedorn, 2002). The ways in which bereaved participants in study 1 understood and experienced time owed much to their membership of a particular society and at a particular stage in that society's development; that is, temporal knowledge is socially and historically contextually dependent. Research participants used their everyday temporal knowledge to make sense of their experiences during the process of their person's dying and their bereavement. Time of death experiences are, therefore, also socially constructed, as are attempts to measure and record the time of death, as discussed in Chapter 5.

Some of the key features of the temporal constructs drawn on in this chapter in the discussion of research participants' experiences are noted in Table 3.

Table 3. Temporal Constructs Used in Understanding the Experience of Time of Death.

Temporal Construct	Key Features
Timescape	Encompasses the different facets of time which go to make up an experience. Includes a range of temporal features, such as temporality, tempo, timing, time sequence and others. (see Adam, 2004, p. 144)
Calendar and clock time	Time as delineated on timepieces and calendars
Time frame	Period of time within which an event occurs. In experiential terms, infrequently described by reference to clocks and calendars but more often by the use of descriptors such as 'before' or 'after' (e.g. before and after the person died)
Fluid time	Time subject to processes of change and flux (see Bauman, 2005)
Liminal time	Time when someone is in transition between two significant states or statuses (see Turner, 1969)
Expanded present	When a moment in time expands to occupy a much longer period, particularly as applied to the present (see Baraitser, 2017)
Observed (witnessed) time	When the bereaved person is present for the death, witnesses it and realises that it has occurred
Unobserved (unwitnessed) time	When the bereaved person misses the death, whether through not being present beside the dying person or through a lack of realisation that the death has occurred

Grief Responses to Bereavement

Participants' responses to the death of their person and how they perceived the time of their death were individual, yet they were also socially and culturally informed (Walter, 1999). What is considered socially acceptable and appropriate practice is fluid, such that it is constantly changing. The flash mob dance at the funeral in Bristol, described in Chapter 3, would have been unthinkable until recently, as would the idea of holding a funeral for yourself while you are still alive.[1]

---

[1]ITV News, 2023, 'I want to forgive myself for abandoning everyone': Why are more people attending their own funeral? https://www.itv.com/news/2023-08-12/why-im-thinking-about-attending-my-own-funeral-while-alive?utm_medium=Social&utm_source=Twitter#Echobox=1691828977

Shared understandings of time gave participants a starting point for reflecting on their views about the time when their person died. Those shared understandings offered a framework within which participants could place their experiences in relation to time and death and construct a suitable narrative. It is also the case, however, that shared understandings provided a framework within which the data analysis was conducted. The researcher is part of the social setting and, while alert to the social construction of time and death, is not immune to the operation of social norms and expectations. The narratives of time of death which have been developed in this book are, therefore, socially and culturally informed.

Conclusion

The Baker family narratives, about the time when Melanie died, demonstrate the complexity involved when we endeavour to limit people's experience to a clock and calendar definition of time of death. Bereaved participants who took part in study 1 all had individual and different experiences, but the temporal underpinnings of those experiences involved shared understandings and embedded knowledge of how time works. The following chapter will consider the notion of the social construction of time of death and the implications for answering the question 'when is the time of death?'

Chapter 7

The Social Construction of the Time of Death

Introduction

The purpose of this chapter is to draw on the empirical data, the literature and the discussions of the previous chapters in order to think about the social construction of time in relation to the time of death in a little more depth. A theme running throughout the book is the suggestion that in order to answer the question 'when is the time of death?', it is important to know something of the broader context within which the question is being asked. This chapter builds upon five claims previously made in the book in order to assist with this task.

The first of these claims is that time, as understood and utilised by humans, is a social construction which is produced and reproduced as people go about their quotidian lives. Humans use time that is collectively produced as a way of organising experiences relative to other experiences and other people. The second claim is that the way in which time is known and used is not only a construct, but that it is one which is dependent on social and historical context; how time is understood and perceived varies across time and place. The third argument is that the meanings which death holds, and what counts as signs of death's occurrence, also change over time and place. The fourth claim is that time of death, as it is understood in 21st century United Kingdom, is also, therefore, a social construction. This is followed by the fifth argument, that there are power relations at play in the construction of times, including of times in relation to death. As a social construction, time is not neutral and there are individuals and groups who have more say in how time is conceived and utilised at an institutional level. Such individuals are also more likely to have a greater degree of control over their own time and its disbursement.

The knowledge and understanding that people have about time comes through familiarity with the constructs. No one would wish to grapple with the process of defining the concept of time every day in order to work out if they are going to be late for work, or whether it is more impolite to arrive early or late at a party. Temporal constructs offer a shorthand way of dealing with what is a complex

Time of Death, 99–111
Copyright © 2024 Glenys Caswell
Published under exclusive licence by Emerald Publishing Limited
doi:10.1108/978-1-80455-005-220241007

concept, and we are so familiar with them that we take them for granted and rarely question the nature of time and how our lives are impacted by it. As Chapter 2 revealed, it has been argued that time may not exist but whether or not that is the case, people behave as if time were real and it is an inextricable part of the organisation of daily lives and deaths.

Some faith systems question the existence and nature of death, promoting instead a belief that mortal human life on earth is simply the precursor to eternal life in another realm. The possibility has also been put forward that what we believe is life has no reality because humans are simply participants in a computer simulation and they have no existence outside the virtual world (Francis, 2014). Addressing the nature of such beliefs is not the concern here, for what matters is that people believe time and death exist outside their own minds and, therefore, behave as if they both have objective existence. The intention here is, rather, to address the question of when it is that people die within the context of a 21st century social setting.

Time is not the only complex concept at play here, death is also not straightforward. This chapter is written from the perspective that people die not once, but twice in that they undergo both bodily and social deaths. As was noted in Chapter 3, death is a process of change. Bodies experience continual change throughout their lives and as they move towards older age, illness and dying. Even after death, processes of change continue as the body decomposes. People also experience change in their relationships and the routines of their lives, including as they die themselves or experience the death of someone about whom they care.

This chapter begins with a brief reprise of the discussions contained in Chapters 2 to 6 before going on to consider time as a construct which is contextually dependent and the context of death as bodily and social death. Next to be considered will be time of death as a 21st century construct. The final section of this chapter will bring together the five forms of death and the relevant temporal constructs which individuals use to organise their experiences.

Reprise: Discussion of Time

Time, as has been noted at various points in this book so far, is a mystery. It is mysterious because we humans do not understand what it is, nor how it works or even whether it has an independent existence outside human consciousness. Human lives appear to be subject to the exigencies of time, constantly moving, changing and producing ideas. There are, however, thinkers who have suggested that this may be a factor of the human brain, and that the apparent shifting through time is caused by activity in the brain itself, or by movement and change taking place in the world (Nail, 2022; Tallis, 2016; Young, 2022). The ways in which humans perceive and experience time are socially and culturally dependent, with a multiplicity of time narratives devised and utilised for the purpose. Time in the global north is largely considered to be linear, with the past, present and future on a continuum. Increasingly accurate timepieces have been invented and developed to measure this linear time which, alongside calendars, enables the accurate measuring and recording of time. This in turn supports the efficient carrying out of a range of scheduled activities upon which advanced capitalist societies depend. Despite the knowledge that time is linear and that the past cannot be revisited, however, people living in such social settings are temporally sophisticated and know that how they experience time may well appear to contradict its supposed linearity.

The argument here is that time is a social construct, one which is continually produced and reproduced. It is one which all societies utilise, but in differing ways so that it is contextually dependent and cannot necessarily be read identically in different social settings. There are power relations at play in the construction of times and the ways in which they operate in a social setting (Nowotny, 1994).

Reprise: Discussion of Death

Like time, death is also something of a mystery, although one definite is that all embodied creatures must die. Humans are unusual in the animal kingdom in that they have awareness of their mortality. This awareness has been blamed for causing fear of death, alongside efforts to delay or defer death, and attempts to avoid it completely. There are two kinds of death to which humans are subject. One is social death, which refers to the time at which a person ceases to be an active agent in the lives of other people (Mulkay & Ernst, 1991). This can occur simultaneously with the death of the person's body, before it or afterwards. Social death is a status which is often imposed on a group by others. For example, it was first described by Sudnow (1967), who was writing about the way in which medical professionals sometimes treated their dying patients as if they were already dead. It is also, however, possible for individuals to withdraw from contact with others and so impose a period of social death upon themselves (Caswell, 2022).

The death of the body is the other form of death to which humans succumb. Biological death is a process and there are a variety of definitions of such death extant in the 21st century. A person, for example, is dead when a qualified and trained person certifies that they are dead, or at the point of irreversibility when their body is shutting down and it is impossible that the person as they were known by others can ever return to life. The death of the body at a cellular, or physiological, level is different again, and it is possible for the body to be kept alive for periods of time by technology.

Integral to the concept of death is change. The living body changes to become a dead one and processes of change continue through decay and decomposition. Change is also integral to shifting relationships between the living, the dying and the deceased, and thus integral to the concept of social death.

Reprise: Discussion of Death and Time

The time of biological death is tricky to define unless witnessed by a trained observer. When a death is unobserved, it can be difficult to identify when it occurred, given that the pace of change is different for each dead body, depending upon factors within the corpse itself and in the outside environment. People who are approaching the end of their lives experience time differently, so that it may appear to be suspended or slowed right down, and those caring for the terminally ill may also find that time behaves erratically compared to how it usually does. All these factors combine to make defining the time of death in a simple and straightforward way a challenge.

Time of death, as time itself, is a social construction. It is used as a way of organising experiences which occur at or around the end of a life. There are power relations at work in relation to the construction of time of death, just as there are in relation to the definition and utilisation of time itself. The state, for example, legislates on what it requires in terms of recording the deaths of its citizens and medicine has the power to say when a person has died.

Reprise: Measuring Time of Death

Since the 19th century, data have been collected by the state in the United Kingdom on its individual citizens. In the 21st century, all deaths must be recorded by law and the information required includes who died, the cause of their death and the date when the death was certified by a medically qualified practitioner. The state collects such data for a number of reasons, including from an expressed desire to decrease the number of deaths which occur, to enable the planning of services and to support research carried out by various organisations and individuals. The key factor for the gathering of state statistics is that they should be reliable, and this is achieved by requiring that the date of death is recorded as the date of certification; this obviates the need to try to discover when the death occurred in difficult situations such as when the dying went unnoticed at the time. In forensic cases, where a person may have been illegally killed by someone else, it is desirable to pin down the time, as well as the date, but this is hard to do using only physical and biological factors. The collection of such statistics, and the manner in which they are recorded, can be read not just as a means of benefiting the population but also as a means of controlling individuals and supporting the politically desired status quo.

Reprise: Experiencing Time of Death

Research participants who took part in study 1 were temporally sophisticated individuals. They had not thought about the temporal elements of their experience when their person was dying, yet they offered narratives of that experience in which time was embedded. Their person underwent biological death, but this was not felt as an isolated moment for the bereaved participants. They were existing in an expanded present where time was fluid, and they were occupying a liminal emotional and temporal space. While they knew that the time of clocks and calendars continued, it ceased to have relevance for them temporarily as they were consumed by their experience of bereavement.

Time as a Construct

The case was argued in Chapter 2 for time as a social construct. Time is something which may, or may not, exist but which generations of societies and civilisations have produced and adapted to such an extent that it is an integral part of social and individual life. We take time for granted and use it without considering what it is and how it works (Berger & Luckmann, 1967; Luckmann, 1991).

There are power implications in the ways in which time is constructed. The more powerful groups in a society have the ability to set the temporal agenda for the state and decide how it works, which then has an impact on the wider population. For example, legal decisions about time in relation to hours of work and education, the hours during which resources and facilities such as consumer goods, transport and health and social care can be accessed are under the government's purview. The Pensions Act of 2014, for example, brought into being by the UK government increased women's retirement age in line with that of men, and is gradually increasing the age at which both women and men will receive their state pension to 67.[1] Prior to the Act, men received their state pension at age 65, women at the age of 60. The age at which older people can claim their state pension, based upon contributions paid during their working lives, is thus increased by government decision. Government also have the potential power to change how clock time is measured, by altering practice during the autumn and spring when, currently, clocks are put back by an hour in the autumn and forward by an hour in the spring (Hussey, 2021). Choices for legislation that any government makes, of course, are subject to many influences and factors outside the legislative setting. It is usually the case, however, that ordinary citizens do not have access to the decision-making processes and do not feel that they have influence (Patel & Quilter-Pinner, 2022). Individuals are, however, affected by the decisions that present and past lawmakers have instituted into law.

How much time an individual has outside their working day depends upon decisions made by many others, including lawmakers who set the legally acceptable hours for the working week and employers who implement these laws. The ways in which individuals use that time outside work relies not only on the choices that they make themselves but also on the relationships and responsibilities they may have within their household and family (Cornwell et al., 2019; Vagni, 2022). Research exploring time use in relation to social stratification in Britain between 1983 and 2015 reveals a complex and changing picture. Women and men in the upper classes are less likely to be employed in paid work during the weekend than those of the working classes, and working class women are more likely to work for pay at the weekend than their male counterparts (Vagni, 2022).

The temporal structure to which individuals are subject is what Berger and Luckmann (1967, p. 41) describe as 'coercive'. There are social rules of time which dictate that events should occur in a certain order so that children are educated

---

[1]UK Government, Pensions Act 2014: https://www.legislation.gov.uk/ukpga/2014/19/contents

and socialised into society, adults should work, older adults retire and then die. The importance of this relationship of power with regard to time here is that it is the powerful groups who have established ways in which the bodies of dead citizens, and others who die within the state boundaries, must be managed. There may be legal sanctions for not adhering to these regulations. For example, a person may be prosecuted for preventing the burial of a body (Jones & Quigley, 2016) or for not registering a death in good time.[2] There is a legal duty to dispose of a corpse in an appropriate manner, but there are limitations on when and how this may be done, so that in cases where cause of death is uncertain and the death becomes a coroner's case, it is the coroner who decides when the death can be registered, and when a funeral can take place.[3]

Time as Contextually Dependent

As time is a social construct, established and developed by generations of humans living in society, with the most powerful groups and individuals having most influence, it is important also to note that what time is depends upon the specific context. While all societies have a concept of time, what that concept is varies, as was discussed in Chapter 2. There are many crossovers and similarities, between the ways in which societies at different periods conceive of time, but there are also divergences. The Chinese and Gregorian calendars differ, so that how each year is described and recognised is different in each. The Chinese calendar operates on a 12 year cycle in which years are named after animals (Kumaar, 2022). Thus the year that is numbered as 2023 in the Gregorian calendar is the year of the Rabbit. However, there are international agreements about time which facilitate the operations of a global society. Universal Coordinated Time has been in operation since the 1960s, which sets a standard in terms of time and date by international agreement so that countries from different parts of the world and with different perspectives on time can coordinate activities.[4]

How time is perceived will impact on how time of death is considered and how it is measured, if such measurement takes place. Prior to the extensive use of timepieces among the general population, the timing of a death was likely to be only by the day. The occurrence of a death may have been noted to coincide with a saint's day perhaps, or people may have retained a personal memory that it happened before nightfall. Instant access to time and date for much of the world's population appears to make it easier to note and record when someone dies. It is reasonably straightforward for historians to document the story of public timepieces. Big Ben, for example, the clock in the Elizabeth Tower at the Houses of

---

[2]Blackstone Solicitors, 'What happens if you don't register a death within five days?', 2021: https://blackstonesolicitorsltd.co.uk/category/news/what-happens-if-you-dont-register-a-death-within-5-days/

[3]UK Government, When a death is reported to the coroner: https://www.gov.uk/after-a-death/when-a-death-is-reported-to-a-coroner

[4]UTC Time Now, 2016–2023, https://www.utctime.net/

Parliament in London, was built on the site of the first chiming public clock in England, which had been introduced into operation in 1367.[5]

Charting the history of the use of personal timepieces and the ways in which clock time began to influence the temporal practices of individuals is, however, much more difficult (Glennie & Thrift, 2009). Glennie and Thrift (2009, p. 408) suggest that the 14th century saw the use of clock times as a regular part of temporal practice in England and Wales, and that by the end of the century, clocks were frequently used in working practice. By 1500, telling the time had become usual practice, and it was common by the end of the 18th century to be asked the time in the street.

Death in Context

Each person dies twice, undergoing both their physical and their social deaths. Each of these deaths is a process rather than event, so that it cannot be fully represented by an instant on the clock.

Death of the Body

The human body is a biological organism, so that at its most basic level, the death of the organism is a biological process. There is a point at which the process whereby organ shutdown becomes irreversible, and this could be noted if a trained observer is present, but non-specialists often fail to realise that death has occurred, or it may be that there is no one present, and so the death is unwitnessed. It is also the case that energy remains in the body's cells for a short time and physiological, or cell, death takes place after the body shuts down as a viable organism. This is as Dr Hamilton described and as Azevedo and Othero (2020) argue in their paper. The death of the body, as a process, thus takes place over a period of time, and the legal declaration as to when the death happened can occur minutes or even years after biological death has occurred. When bodily death occurs, those who know and care about the dying person experience the time differently and in ways that diverge from clock-based linear time.

Social Death

It is just about impossible to place a clock and calendar time on social death. The term is used here to mean the point at which people who knew the dead person finally cease to take them into account. A person is not socially dead when the living speak to them, talk about them, consider their views when making choices and so on. The maintenance of an individual's social existence after their biological death requires that someone living knows the deceased person and references what they know of them and is according to them a limited degree of social

---

[5]A brief history of Big Ben and Elizabeth Tower, 2022, https://www.parliament.uk/about/living-heritage/building/palace/big-ben/building-clock-tower/key-dates-/

agency. The survivor may have a view of the deceased person that is different to that of others' and of the dead individual themselves when they were alive, but this perspective comes from first-hand knowledge and a personal relationship. Some historical figures will have had a lasting impact on the lives of many who live in the times after they themselves have died. However, they are socially dead because there is no one living who had interactions with them, and any knowledge that we have of them is mediated through generations of historical scholarship and stories, rather than through personal experience. The relationship between Alison and her daughter Rachel, described in Chapter 6, illustrates the way in which it is possible for a bereaved person to maintain a relationship with their deceased person in such a way that the deceased individual has an ongoing degree of social agency, however limited that may be.

When a person undergoes social death prior to the death of their body, it is possible that the legal declaration of their time of death may be days, weeks, months or even years after their bodily death. In this situation, they have already ceased to be an active agent in the lives of others, so the death of their body was their final death. The post-death processes which must be carried out will cause notice to be taken of the individual, but they will not be accorded any degree of agency and, with their funeral and the final handling of any possessions which they left behind, they are likely to depart back into obscurity.

Time of Death as 21st Century Construct

Time of death is a social construction. As such, consideration of the different ways in which it can be applied in 21st century United Kingdom can offer an insight into perceptions of death, as well as time. Five key forms of death will be considered in turn, and the temporal constructs which are used to articulate and make sense of them will be discussed. The forms of death are bodily death, legal declaration of death, experiencing the death of someone of personal importance, socially proscribed death and social death (Table 4).

Time of Bodily Death

Bodily death signals the end of the person's existence as an embodied individual, and the end of their embodied relationships with other people who are still alive. The point at which the body ceases to be a viable organism, the point of decease (Azevedo & Othero, 2020), is often recognised by skilled professionals and sometimes by family members who are in attendance at the bedside. On these occasions, when the moment of decease is witnessed and noticed, it is possible to assign a calendar date and a clock time to the death.

Deaths are not, however, always witnessed by someone who recognises that the death has occurred. Healthcare professionals are rarely able to stay with a dying person, and family members who do so will not always be aware that the death has occurred. It is also the case that even when family and friends are maintaining a vigil beside their dying person, the death can take place when they

Table 4. Forms of Death and Their Associated Temporal Constructs.

Form of Death	Temporal Constructs
Bodily death: Biological, physiological, organs cease to function, body dies at cellular level	Calendar and clock time Time frame Unobserved time
Legal declaration of death by qualified medical practitioner	Calendar and clock time
Experiencing death of someone of personal importance	Timescape Calendar and clock time Time frame Fluid time Liminal time Witnessed (observed) time Unwitnessed (unobserved) time Expanded time
Socially proscribed death	Unobserved time Unknowable time Time frame Time restored
Social death	Unobserved time Unknowable time

have left the bedside to make a phone call, perhaps, or to get a cup of coffee or something to eat, as was noted in Chapter 6. The death can occur, that is, during unobserved time as when Richard Hayden's wife died while he was in the room with her, but asleep.

In many cases when death happens during unobserved time, the dying person has been cared for during the last phase of their life. The likelihood in this situation is that, while they may have been on their own at the moment of decease, they will not have been alone for a long period of time. Their death occurred during what was probably a short time frame, encompassing the period between when they were last seen alive and the time at which they were found to have died (Adam, 2004).

Forensic pathologist, Dr Hamilton, spoke about the difficulties of assigning a time of death through the examination of the dead body, and suggested that the most accurate way of assessing time of death would be with a time frame between when the person was last seen alive and when they were found dead. In addition, he noted that the use of technologies, such as CCTV, which may have recorded relevant information, or items such as Fitbits and smart watches which may note when the wearer stops moving, could be helpful in narrowing down the time at which a person died.

What is clear from this brief discussion is that it is not an easy matter to assign an accurate time of death in most cases when someone dies. This is not about timepieces and calendars, as we have very accurate timepieces available which can measure time down to fractions of a second and the calendar in the United Kingdom has been Gregorian for centuries so that people are familiar with it. In the 21st century, many people have access to smart phones and computers which offer immediate, and accurate, information on date and time. The difficulty stems, not from being unable to be precise enough about the time but from not being in a position to know when that time arrives. Too often, the moment of death is not witnessed, not noticed or those present do not realise that the death has occurred.

Legal Declaration of Death

In the United Kingdom, it is a legal requirement for each person's death to be certified by a qualified medical practitioner. They complete a standard death certificate form which, among other things, includes date of certification. The person's medical notes are also likely to include the time at which the death is certified, and the medical certificate which must be completed when the body is going to be cremated also requires a time of death.[6] The key point here is that the date recorded is not the date of death, but the date when the body is found and on which death is certified to have happened. This can be the same day on which person died, but could also be many years after their death. The temporal construct utilised here is that of calendar and clock time.

Experiencing the Death of Someone of Personal Importance

For people who are emotionally and socially close to the dying person, the time of death is a more complex concept. Research participants spoke about their experience during the time when their person was dying in a way that is described here in terms of timescapes (Adam, 2004). They spoke, that is, of the entirety of their experience, including the moments around the death, but also including the period prior to and after the death. Participants were all aware that time as represented on clocks and calendars continued, and some noted clock times, as Bob Carstairs did in his belief that his father had died at three o'clock in the afternoon. The date of death was important to participants, even if they were less clear about the time of day. Mary Blythe, for example, was clear about the date on which her husband had died, but uncertain as to exactly when his funeral had taken place. For Melanie Baker's family, the day of her death was always memorable, as she died on her own daughter's birthday.

---

[6]Cremation medical certificate, England and Wales, 2023: https://www.gov.uk/government/publications/cremation-medical-certificate

Despite the knowledge that linear clock and calendar time continued, however, their perception was that time behaved differently during the period when their person was dying and in the aftermath of the death. People going through the process which would leave them bereaved were in a temporal space which can be described as liminal (Turner, 1969). They were in a place where they were about-to-be bereaved, but were not quite yet, and even once the death of their person had happened, they would not immediately feel their change in status from spouse or child or sibling to that of a widowed or orphaned person or bereaved sibling.

The moment at which a person dies is perceived as important, with an expectation that their family should be beside them when this occurs. Some research participants were with their person when they died, and some were not. However, although all would have liked to be there and aware of what was happening, that moment of decease (Azevedo & Othero, 2020) was experienced as part of an expanded present (Baraitser, 2017). The time of death for those who had experienced a bereavement can best be described as a time frame, but one with a beginning and end which may not be accountable in clock and calendar terms. Time during the process of becoming, and being, bereaved was fluid for research participants (Bauman, 2005). It did not necessarily maintain its linearity and sometimes it grew to become almost endless or shrank to virtually nothing.

One way in which the fluidity of time was experienced by participants was through the ongoing relationships which some of them took care to maintain with their deceased person. Alison Taylor, for example, made conscious efforts not just to keep the memory of her daughter Rachel alive, but also to ensure that something of the contribution that she believed Rachel would have made to the world was still possible.

Socially Proscribed Death

There are some deaths which are beyond the social pale. People who are the victims of genocide or other crimes against humanity die in a time which is unobserved and unknown to anyone beyond the circle of their killers. The likelihood is that there are many multiple graves in existence where the bodies of individual people killed in this way remain, while some countries have used the practice of dumping bodies at sea so that they are very unlikely to be found. The people who cared about those who went missing may know what happened and suspect the fate of their person, but in these cases, the time of the death remains unobserved and unknowable. There are some instances, however, as noted in Chapters 3 and 5, where the reality of crimes against humanity has come to light and graves have been discovered. When this occurs, efforts are made to identify the bodies and return them to their families (Moon, 2016, 2019, 2020).

When these efforts are successful and the deceased individuals are reunited with their families, this is described here as time restored in relation to the when of the person's death. There is no possibility of getting back the last weeks, days and hours of the person's life for their family to spend with them; there is no possibility of sharing the immediate mourning period; there is no possibility of having the appropriate post-death rituals at the appropriate time. But when efforts to identify the bodies of the deceased are successful and they have sur-viving families who can be found, then there is the chance of restoring the body to the family so that they can carry out their rituals as they see fit. The timelines of the family and their deceased member will realign.

The other form of socially proscribed death to feature here is that of people who die alone. As has been noted, it is not uncommon for people to be alone at the moment of their decease, in cases when they have been cared for and accompanied throughout their final illness and in the last hours of their lives. But there are also instances where people who live alone also die alone at home, and sometimes in these cases the person's body may not be found for an extended period of time (Caswell, 2022). When someone dies alone in this way, their death occurs at an unobserved and unknowable time, for they were unnoticed in their lives and so in their deaths. When their bodies are found, however that might come about, it is possible to suggest that their death occurred during a time frame. The end of the time frame is, of course, when their body was discovered, but often the beginning of that frame will be harder to assess. The dates on newspapers or television listings magazines, use by dates on food in their fridge, notes made on a calendar, or when a neighbour last saw them may offer clues. However, unless there is evidence that someone else was involved in their death, there will be no effort expended in trying to narrow down this time frame, and their death will be recorded as having occurred when it was certified by a suitably qualified medical practitioner. That is, their date of death will be recorded as the date on which their body was discovered.

Social Death

Some of the people who die alone at home are found when someone else notices that they are not engaging in their usual activities. Neighbours notice that they are not going out or putting the bins out, relatives realise they have not received a phone call or text for a long time. In some cases, though, a person lives alone and has few social contacts with other people, so that there is no one to notice their absence from their routines. Their death is likely to be discovered when entry is forced into their home because of unpaid bills, or because there is a water leak which negatively impacts neighbours, or something similar. In such instances, the individual may have chosen to enter a state of social death while still biologically alive, in that they have ceased to have any active engagement with other people and thus exhibit no agency in the lives of others.

Undergoing a process of social death, whenever this occurs relative to bodily death, is invisible and happens at a time which is both unobserved and unknown. Everyone who lives must die both a bodily and a social death. Most individuals live within networks of relationships and the timing of their social death depends upon those relationships. It can happen post-death when a bereaved survivor not only maintains an ongoing relationship with the deceased person based upon memory but also accords to the deceased person an element of agency within that relationship. The when of the social death of a person accorded such ongoing agency is impossible to know, just as the when of a social death which occurs before bodily death is unknowable.

Conclusion

A range of temporal constructs are required in order to explore when death occurs in its different forms. Whatever form of death is under consideration, time of death is a social construct, and the implications of this for answering the question 'when is the time of death?' will be the subject of the next, and final, chapter.

Chapter 8

Conclusion

H. G. Wells published his novella, *The Time Machine*, in 1895. This was innovative fiction, the first in which a person travelled in time, other than by living through it in the usual fashion. The story itself continues to fascinate and to inspire other stories told using different media over a 100 years after its initial publication (Firchow, 2004). The tale is told by a Narrator, and the main character, who is identified only as the Time Traveller, builds a machine which allows him to travel through time. He travels far into the future and then returns to tell a group of his friends whom he has invited to dinner at his home, about his experiences. They are, not surprisingly, sceptical. The Narrator returns to the Time Traveller's home at a later date to speak further with him on the subject. He is unable to do so because when he arrives, the Traveller is leaving on his time machine, camera in hand doubtless with the intention of returning with photographic proof. Despite the Narrator waiting, the Time Traveller does not return and has not done so by the end of the story. The Narrator wonders whether he is trapped in some far distant time, whether he has decided to stay in another century or whether the Time Traveller is dead (Wells, 1895/2005).

The Time Machine was the product of Wells' imagination, and it opened up ideas about time and whether it might not be as fixed as we usually perceive it to be. Creative writers in varied media continue to tell stories about travellers in time and members of the public continue to consume them. Time travel appears as if it might be possible given that when we look up at the stars in the night sky, we are looking back into the past (Devereaux, 2022). Travelling in time also seems to offer much including, perhaps, the possibility of cheating death. The servant who lived in Baghdad was unable to evade death by fleeing through space to Samarra, but might it have been possible by fleeing through time as well (Maugham, 1933/2017)? For, as discussed in Chapter 4, the fact of death appears to make little sense without the limits placed on life by time.

The intention here is to pull together the threads from the previous chapters in order to consider the overall contribution made to understanding the concept 'time of death'. It starts by offering a brief reminder of the lines of argument, before going on to consider some of the factors that should be taken into account when assigning a time to a death and then asking what if time does not exist? This chapter ends by revisiting the question, 'when is the time of death' for the final time.

Time of Death, 113–119

Copyright © 2024 Glenys Caswell

Published under exclusive licence by Emerald Publishing Limited

doi:10.1108/978-1-80455-005-220241008

Argument So Far

Time of death is a concept which, as soon as we start to unpack what it is and what it means, is elusive. Throughout the book, the argument has been presented that this difficulty in definition comes about because both time and death defy simple description. It is unclear what time is or even whether it exists outside the human conception of it. Time, therefore, including time of death, is a social construction which is defined through social use and people's perception. The suggestion is also offered that each person undergoes two deaths, a bodily death and a social death, and each of these deaths is a process not a one-off event. Time is a concept that individuals and groups use to organise their experiences as part of the effort to make sense of them and hold them together in a coherent way. This includes the experiences which we have around dying and death, as presenting events in temporal order helps us to bring order to the apparent chaos of dying.

What counts as the time of any particular death cannot, therefore, always be reduced to a time on the clock and a date on the calendar. It depends upon a variety of factors, including who it is that is assigning a time to the death, whether they are concerned with bodily or social death, whether or not the death was witnessed, the reason for the need to assign a time and what measure of time they are using.

Broadly speaking, there are two interest groups in relation to time of death which have been discussed throughout the book. First, there are the institutions, such as the state, medicine and the legal system. The state has the power to set policy and law on relevant issues including end of life care for the population and legal requirements relating to the registering of deaths and the disposal of dead bodies. The legal system involves a wide range of professionals, including lawyers, coroners, medical doctors, police and registrars. Their roles encompass such tasks as the certifying and registration of deaths, including how and when they happened, ensuring compliance with the regulatory systems and examining deaths which are deemed suspicious or of unknown cause. Institutional interests rarely take account of the emotionality and relationality of death, which is, rather, where the interests of individuals lie.

The second group with an interest in time in relation to death are those individuals who have been bereaved. This potentially includes every member of the population, as everyone is likely to experience a bereavement at some point in their lives. Their interest is personal, emotional and stems from their relationships with other people.[1] Bereaved research participants in study 1 were keen to be with their person when they died, although this was not always possible. They spoke about the death of the body as the person dying, but in most cases, they also maintained an ongoing bond with the individual after their death. The deceased

---

[1]People can, of course, experience loss and bereavement in circumstances other than through the death of a person who is important to them. The death of a pet can be a significant loss, for example (see Hess-Holden et al., 2017). The focus here, however, is solely on bereavement through the death of a person.

person's social death thus took place at a later time than their bodily death. Dates were important, and the anniversary of the death would later be recalled with emotion. For some participants, specific anniversaries, such as birthdays or the first Father's Day, after death became of key importance for remembering. On the whole, however, the time of death was part of an expanded present. Participants expressed a lack of awareness about time, yet this was coupled with a temporal fluency which suggests the embedded nature of time in human lives and the ways in which time is used as an organising concept in relation to experiences.

Assigning a Time of Death

Assigning a time to a death is not a straightforward matter, and there are a number of factors which impact how any death is defined in temporal terms.

Time of Death as a Form of Communication

As discussed in Chapter 2, time can be viewed as a form of communication. A recent analysis of neolithic cave paintings posited the idea that they were calendars and forms of communication which contained calendrical information for others in the nomadic community (Bacon et al., 2023). In the 21st century, time continues to be a form of communication. As individuals, we may communicate with our future selves through the use of diary and journal entries. We may communicate temporally with others, for example, through the sending of electronic calendar invites or through dates on letters and the dates and times embedded in emails and online posts.

In some instances, the time attributed to a death, or when there is no time given, can also be a form of communication. In the case of lone deaths, for example, when someone dies alone at home and the time of death is recorded as the date on which the body was found, even when the time lapse between death and discovery was clearly years long. This can be read as the communication of an institutional message from the state about the worth of a person who would die such a death and the need for such a death to be regularised and brought back under control through the exercise of post-death legal processes (Caswell, 2022).

For victims of genocide and other heinous crimes, the lack of acknowledgement that the death has occurred and when and how it took place also sends a message. The people who ordered and carried out the murder have tried to obliterate the deceased person from existence, communicating through the lack of a time of death and the concealment of the person's body their supposed lack of worth as a person. However, such efforts are doomed to eventual failure because the lost and murdered people are remembered by those who knew and cared about them and efforts to discover what happened to them will continue, often resulting in the discovery and identification of their bodies and their return to their families (Moon, 2016, 2019, 2020).

Sometimes, therefore, the time of death, or the lack of a time of death, sends a message from those with the power in a social setting.

Power Relations

Since the 19th century, for countries in the United Kingdom, time of death has been a legal construct and one in which the implementation relies upon qualified and licensed individuals carrying out specific tasks in relation to all deaths which occur in the United Kingdom. It also requires that members of the public play their part in the registration of deaths system and, allied to that, in arranging and paying for a legally appropriate method of disposal. The state legislates for individuals to provide the relevant information and for designated professionals to undertake the associated tasks as a way of gathering population level data about deaths. These form the basis of the official mortality statistics held by the state. The state also decides what counts as the official time when someone is dead, and that is when the official declaration of death takes place. As previously noted, this can happen any time from minutes after the person's bodily death to years later. The processes at work here are those of state power, for individuals may choose not to adhere to the rules, but they risk discovery and the imposition of a penalty (Higgs, 2004; Jones & Quigley, 2016).

The Power of Social Norms

It is possible for time to be used collaboratively and in an egalitarian fashion, such as when friends arrange to meet for a social occasion at a time that is convenient for all. However, even in social situations, the temporal choices which individuals make and the experiences they have may be influenced by social expectations and norms. For bereaved people, those who are most significantly affected by a death, the moment of death is loaded with significance. There is a cultural script, knowledge of which places pressure on family members and other close people to witness the dying process and to accompany the person when they die (Seale, 1998). Participants in study 1 expressed this knowledge, which is in line with the findings from other studies, and most wished to be with their dying person. Some, however, were not present either because they missed the moment for some reason or because they preferred not to witness the death (Caswell et al., 2022; Donnelly & Battley, 2010; Donnelly & Donnelly, 2006; Valentine, 2007).

Embodiment and Social Relations

The relationships which the deceased person had while alive complicate their status once they have undergone bodily death. The living can no longer enjoy the embodied relationship they had with the deceased person, but the ways in which bereavement is viewed have changed. The emphasis in the 21st century is no longer on working through a series of stages and then moving on from the deceased person but, rather, focuses on the maintenance of continuing bonds (Klass & Steffen, 2018). The living are thus acknowledged as maintaining ongoing relationships with their dead and in some instances that leads to the dead person being accorded a small measure of social agency, that is, they are not yet socially dead. Bereaved participants in study 1 maintained relationships with their deceased person, continuing to think and talk about them. However, one impact of biological death is that we will never have those embodied interactions with the person again; we will never hug them, never have face to face conversations, never have social occasions or share a laugh as we had before. Their body is gone, and we knew them and interacted with them through their bodies.

The Technological Obscuring of Death

Technology offers a range of ways in which death can either be hidden or deferred. Life support systems can keep the biological body functioning past the point of irreversible brain damage, while technology such as defibrillators can be employed to obscure a death in public space and re-site it into the private sphere (Timmons et al., 2010). For some, the lure of a future in which their body can be revived so as to live again leads them to opt for cryogenic preservation (Dein, 2022). The online world also offers ways of staying present in the world post physical death, through the use of social media accounts and facilities which permit the setting up of messages to be sent after your death (Bassett, 2018; Kasket, 2012, 2019).

All these factors can impact how an individual's time of death is perceived by others, and how it is recorded. They also highlight the necessity of using different temporal constructs in relation to the different forms of dying as was previously identified in Chapter 7.

What If Time Does Not Exist?

If it should turn out that time does not exist, how would it impact people's lives and deaths? In going about our daily lives, we tend to assume that we know what time is and how it works. We use this knowledge as the basis for our temporal lives and regimes, yet we are wrong and we do not know; we do not have the key to time's mystery. If it should turn out that Baron et al. (2022) are right in their theorising and that time does not exist, then the impact on people's dying would likely be negligible. Processes of human management of the dying and the dead work when we base the temporal aspects of it on false assumptions made about time so that there is no need for it to make any difference if the falsity were proved. Change will continue to occur, with bodies decomposing from the moment of physiological death, and bereaved people will continue to experience grief and mourning in ways which may change continuously.

When Is the Time of Death?

Dying is not a momentary event but a process, which the about-to-be bereaved shares with the dying person. Inevitably, the sharing stops at the moment of decease, the point at which the person they were as an embodied individual acting in the world is irretrievably gone. The very significance of the moment means that it defies capture in one second or minute on a clock. That moment on the clock will return again and again every 12 or 24 hours, but the death will not, for it takes place in the expanded present during which clock time ceases to have relevance. The person who was dying may retain a measure of social agency, but they no longer have an embodied presence in the world.

Data and discussion in Chapter 5 demonstrate that even when attempts are made to measure the time of a death accurately, this is not always possible. Dr Hamilton, the forensic pathologist, alluded to some of the difficulties that he and his colleagues encounter when trying to determine the length of time since death by reference only to the dead body. The way in which the official time of death is recorded for state purposes owes little to when the death occurred. The official time of death is the time when the individual is legally declared to be dead, and this can vary from a few minutes to years after the death, depending upon the circumstances.

There is thus no definitive time of death which can be applied to all deaths. This, as we have seen during the course of the book, comes about because both time and death are complex concepts which are not fully understood. Does this matter? I suggest that it does not. To talk about the time of death may come about from a desire to know and understand when an individual died. But it may also be prompted by a variety of other factors such as, for example, the human desire to categorise and label people and events or the desire to exercise social power.

Concluding Thoughts

This book makes no claim to be telling the full story of the concept 'time of death', rather it is an attempt to open up the discussion and to suggest some possible lines of enquiry. Unpacking the 'time of death' concept is complex because the human relationship with death and time is also complex. The phrase 'time of death' can be read as a shorthand way of referring to a range of experiences which can take place over a period of time, rather than as a definitive reference to when a person's death occurs.

The role of the social sciences is, of course, to explore and challenge taken-for-granted understandings of social practices, including in relation to time and death. At the start of the book, it was suggested that time of death is an important concept for social science disciplines to explore. The bulk of the research carried out in this field is medically based, part of the endeavour to discover the secret to establishing an accurate time since death in forensic cases. This is important, but there is more to what constitutes the time of death than this.

It is important for social science disciplines to research and study time and death because dying is not just about biological events happening to a body, it is a social and relational business, and time of death is about more than trying to pinpoint when a body ceases to function. Data in the book demonstrate that time of death is a social construction, as time itself is a social construction, and when applied to a death, it is also a legal artefact and something which can be construed as an exercise of power relations. Those who care about a dying person do not just experience the time on the clock, as with so many experiences, they find that time does not just go tick, tick with the seconds, it can speed up, slow down, stop and so on. Often, too, the moment of death is missed or obscured, even if there is such a thing as a moment of death.

So answering the question 'when is the time of death?' is tricky. How we answer the question depends upon the circumstances and what we need from the answer. It may be that we are content with a notional time, as Bob Carstairs was in Chapter 6, when his father died. It may be that a particular death is too big and important to contain in a moment, as research participants found when describing the death of their important person. Or it may be that we attempt to fine tune that moment, in order to assign blame to someone else for the death.

Whatever route we take when answering the question, however, it must be remembered that we do not make our choices in isolation, and there are constraints upon the ways we can respond to the question. Time of death is a social construction, and we answer using the narratives we have available to us. As we have seen, there are situations where power relations come into play and influence what is required, or possible, in a response. We must also recall that when we engage with our emotional responses to a death, we are enacting appropriate behaviours as we have learnt them in our social setting.

References

AbouZahr, C., de Savigny, D., Mikkelsen, L., Setel, P. W., Lozano, R., & Lopez, A. D. (2015). Towards universal civil registration and vital statistics systems: The time is now. *The Lancet, 386*, 1407–1418. https://doi.org/10.1016/S0140-6736(15)60170-2

Academy of Medical Royal Colleges. (2008). *A code of practice for the diagnosis and confirmation of death.* https://www.aomrc.org.uk/reports-guidance/ukdec-reports-and-guidance/code-practice-diagnosis-confirmation-death/

Adam, B. (1990). *Time & social theory.* Polity Press.

Adam, B. (1995). *Timewatch.* Polity Press.

Adam, B. (2002). Perceptions of time. In T. Ingold (Ed.), *Companion encyclopedia of anthropology* (2nd ed., pp. 503–526). Routledge.

Adam, B. (2004). *Time.* Polity Press.

Alfsdotter, C., & Petaros, A. (2021). Outdoor human decomposition in Sweden: A retrospective quantitative study of forensic-taphonomic changes and postmortem interval in terrestrial and aquatic settings. *Journal of Forensic Sciences, 66*, 1348–1363. https://doi.org/10.1111/1556-4029.14719

Alipour, J., & Payandeh, A. (2021). Common errors in reporting cause-of-death statement on death certificates: A systematic review and meta-analysis. *Journal of Forensic and Legal Medicine, 82*. https://doi.org/10.1016/j.jflm.2021.102220

Allin, P. (2022). *The role and use of official statistics in measuring wellbeing.* What Works Centre for Wellbeing. https://whatworkswellbeing.org/blog/measuring-wellbeing-population-level-data/

Ang, C.-S. (2023). Life will never be the same: Experiences of grief and loss among older adults. *Current Psychology, 42*, 12975–12987. https://doi.org/10.1007/s12144-021-02595-6

Azevedo, M. A., & Othero, J. C. B. (2020). Human death as a triptych process. *Mortality.* https://doi.org/10.1080/13576275.2020.1756765

Bacon, B., Khatiri, A., Palmer, J., Freeth, T., Pettitt, P., & Kentridge, R. (2023). An upper Palaeolithic proto-writing system and phenological calendar. *Cambridge Archaeological Journal.* https://doi.org/10.1017/S0959774322000415

Baert, P., Morgan, M., & Ushiyama, R. (2022). Existence theory: Outline for a theory of social behaviour. *Journal of Classical Sociology, 22*(1), 7–29. https://doi.org/10.1177/1468795X21998247

Baggini, J. (2018). *How the world thinks.* Granta.

Bailey, C., & Madden, A. (2017). Time reclaimed: Temporality and the experience of meaningful work. *Work, Employment & Society, 31*(1), 3–18. https://doi.org/10.1177/0950017015604100

Baldwin, P. K. (2017). Death Cafés: Death doulas and family communication. *Behavioral Sciences, 7*(26). https://doi.org/10.3390/bs7020026

Baraitser, L. (2017). *Enduring time.* Bloomsbury Academic.

Bardon, A. (2013). *A brief history of the philosophy of time*. Oxford University Press.

Baron, S., Miller, K., & Tallant, J. (2022). *Out of time: A philosophical study of timelessness*. Oxford University Press.

Bassett, D. (2018). Digital afterlives: From social media platforms to Thanabots and beyond. In C. Tandy (Ed.), *Death and anti-death, Vol. 16:200 years after Frankenstein* (pp. 27–38). Ria University Press.

Bastion, M., Baraitser, L., Flexer, M. J., Hom, A. R., & Salisbury, L. (2020). Introduction: The social life of time. *Time & Society, 29*(2), 289–296. https://doi.org/10.1177/0961463X20921674

Basu, J. K., & Adair, T. (2021). Have inequalities in completeness of death registration between states in India narrowed during two decades of civil registration system strengthening? *International Journal for Equity in Health, 20*(195). https://doi.org/10.1186/s12939-021-01534-y

Bauld, L. (2011). *The impact of smoke free legislation in England: Evidence review.* https://www.gov.uk/government/publications/impact-of-smokefree-legislation-evidence-review-march-2011

Bauman, Z. (1992). *Mortality, immortality & other life strategies*. Stanford University Press.

Bauman, Z. (2005). *Liquid life*. Polity Press.

Bauman, Z. (2006). *Liquid Fear*. Polity Press.

Bell, J., Bailey, L., & Kennedy, D. (2015). 'We do it to keep him alive': Bereaved individuals' experiences of online suicide memorials and continuing bonds. *Mortality, 20*(4), 375–389. http://doi.org/10.1080/13576275.2015.1083693

Berger, P. L. (1969). *The sacred canopy*. Anchor Books.

Berger, P., & Luckmann, T. (1967). *The social construction of reality*. Penguin Press.

Bericat, E. (2016). The sociology of emotions: Four decades of progress. *Current Sociology, 64*(3), 491–513. https://doi.org/10.1177/0011392115588355

Bird-David, N., & Israeli, T. (2010). A moment dead, a moment alive: How a situational personhood emerges in the vegetative state in an Israeli hospital unit. *American Anthropologist, 112*(1), 54–65. https://doi.org/10.1111/j.1548-1433.2009.01196.x

Bishop, J. P. (2011). *The anticipatory corpse*. University of Notre Dame Press.

Black, S. (2018). *All that remains a life in death*. Black Swan.

Bluedorn, A. C. (2002). *The human organization of time*. Stanford University Press.

BMA. (2023). *Physician-assisted dying legislation around the world*. https://www.bma.org.uk/advice-and-support/ethics/end-of-life/physician-assisted-dying

Borgstrom, E. (2017). Social death. *QJM: International Journal of Medicine, 110*(1), 5–7. https://doi.org/10.1093/qjmed/hcw183

Bozzaro, C. (2022). Medical technologies, time, and the good life. *History & Philosophy of the Life Sciences, 44*(29). https://doi.org/10.1007/s40656-022-00504-z

Bradbury, M. (1999). *Representations of death*. Routledge.

Brewer, J. D. (2018). Towards a sociology of compromise. In J. D. Brewer, B. C. Hayes, & F. Teeney (Eds.), *The sociology of compromise after conflict* (pp. 1–30). Palgrave Macmillan.

Cameron, A. (2007). The establishment of civil registration in Scotland. *Historical Journal, 50*(2), 377–396. https://doi.org/10.1017/S0018246X07006115

Carrasco, M. A., & Valera, L. (2021). Diagnosing death: The "fuzzy area" between life and decomposition. *Theoretical Medicine and Bioethics*. https://doi.org/10.1007/s11017-021-09541-4

Carvalho, R. G., Capelo, R., & Nunez, D. (2018). Perspectives concerning the future when time is suspended: Analysing inmates' discourse. *Time & Society*, *27*(3), 295–311. https://doi.org/10.1177/0961463X15604533

Caswell, G. (2020). 'A Stark and lonely death': Representations of dying alone in popular culture. In A. Teodorescu & M. H. Jacobsen (Eds.), *Death in contemporary popular culture* (pp. 38–50). Routledge.

Caswell, G. (2021). Dying alone: Exercising a right or transgressing the rules? In S. Westwood (Ed.), *The regulation of the end of life: Death rights* (pp. 205–218). Routledge.

Caswell, G. (2022). *Dying alone: Challenging assumptions*. Palgrave MacMillan.

Caswell, G., & O'Connor, M. (2015). Agency in the context of social death: Dying alone at home. *Contemporary Social Science*, *10*(3), 249–261. https://doi.org/10.1080/21582041.2015.1114663

Caswell, G., & O'Connor, M. (2019). 'I've no fear of dying alone': Exploring perspectives on living and dying alone. *Mortality*, *24*(1), 17–31. http://doi.org/10.1080/13576275.2017.1413542

Caswell, G., & Turner, N. (2020). Ethical challenges in researching and telling the stories of recently deceased people. *Research Ethics*, *17*(2), 162–175. https://doi.org/10.1177/1747016120952503

Caswell, G., Wilson, E., Turner, N., & Pollock, K. (2022). It's not like in the films': Bereaved people's experiences of the deathbed vigil. *OMEGA – Journal of Death and Dying*. https://doi.org/10.1177/00302228221133413

Cave, S. (2013). *Immortality*. Biteback Publishing.

Charmaz, K. (2006). *Constructing grounded theory*. Sage.

Christie, A. (1926/2007). *The murder of Roger Ackroyd*. Harper Collins.

Cipriani, R. (2013). The many faces of social time: A sociological approach. *Time & Society*, *22*(1), 5–30. https://doi.org/10.1177/0961463X12473948

Clark, J. T. (2023). Can we teach undergraduates the history of time? *Time & Society*, *32*(3), 272–279. https://doi.org/10.1177/0961463X221111048

Clarke, C. (2018, September 13). Breaking the taboo: The director who has filmed the moment of death. *The Guardian*. https://www.theguardian.com/film/2018/sep/13/island-documentary-steven-eastwood

Cornwell, B., Gershuny, J., & Sullivan, O. (2019). The social structure of time: Emerging trends and new directions. *Annual Review of Sociology*, *45*, 301–320. https://doi.org/10.1146/annurev-soc-073018-022416

Coveney, P., & Highfield, R. (1991). *The arrow of time*. Flamingo.

Craig, L., & Mullan, K. (2011). How mothers and fathers share childcare: A cross-national time-use comparison. *American Sociological Review*, *76*(6), 834–861. https://doi.org/10.1177/0003122411427673

Danckert, J. A., & Allman, A.-A. A. (2005). Time flies when you're having fun: Temporal estimation and the experience of boredom. *Brain and Cognition*, *59*, 236–245. https://doi.org/10.1016/j.bandc.2005.07.002

Dattani, S. (2023). How are causes of death registered around the world? OurWorldInData.org. https://ourworldindata.org/how-are-causes-of-death-registered-around-the-world

Davies, D. J. (2002). *Death, ritual and belief* (2nd ed.). Continuum.

Degen, M. (2018). Timescapes of urban change: The temporalities of regenerated streets. *The Sociological Review, 66*(5), 1074–1092. https://doi.org/10.1177/0038026118771290

Dehpour, T., & Koffman, J. (2023). Assessment of anticipatory grief in informal caregivers of dependants with dementia: A systematic review. *Aging & Mental Health, 27*(1), 110–123. https://doi.org/10.1080/13607863.2022.2032599

Dein, S. (2022). Cryonics: Science or religion. *Journal of Religion and Health, 61*, 3164–3176. https://doi.org/10.1007/s10943-020-01166-6

Dein, S., & George, R. (2001). The time to die: Symbolic factors relating to the time of death. *Mortality, 6*(2), 201–211. https://doi.org/10.1080/13576270120051857

Devereaux, C. (2022). Most distant star to date spotted – But how much further back in time could we see? *The Conversation.* https://theconversation.com/most-distant-star-to-date-spotted-but-how-much-further-back-in-time-could-we-see-180623

Doig, A. (2022). *This mortal coil.* Bloomsbury.

Donnelly, S., & Battley, J. (2010). Relatives' experiences of the moment of death in a tertiary referral hospital. *Mortality, 15*(1), 81–100. https://doi.org/10.1080/13576270903537641

Donnelly, S. M., & Donnelly, C. (2006). Experience of the moment of death at home. *Mortality, 11*(4), 352–367. https://doi.org/10.1080/13576270600945410

Dorow, S., & Jean, S. (2022). Managing liminal time in the fly-in fly-out work camp. *Human Relations, 75*(4), 834–861. https://doi.org/10.1177/0018726721989792

Dorries, C. (2014). *Coroners' courts* (3rd ed.). Oxford University Press.

Droit-Volet, S. (2019). Time does not fly but slow down in old age. *Time & Society, 28*(1), 60–82. https://doi.org/10.1177/0961463X16656852

Duncan, D. E. (1999). *The calendar.* Fourth Estate.

Evans-Pritchard, E. E. (1939). Nuer time-reckoning. *Africa: Journal of the International African Institute, 12*(2), 189–216. https://doi.org/10.2307/1155085

Fairbairn, C. (2021). *Death certification and medical examiners.* House of Commons Library.

Feynman, R. P. (1955). The value of science. *Engineering and Science, 19*, 13–15. https://archive.org/details/feynman_201604

Firchow, P. (2004). H. G. Wells's time machine: In search of time future – And time past. *The Midwest Quarterly, 45*(2), 123–136.

Foer, J., & Siffre, M. (2008). Caveman: An interview with Michel Siffre. *Cabinet, 30*. https://www.cabinetmagazine.org/issues/30/toc.php

Foulkes, N. (2019). *Time tamed: The remarkable story of humanity's quest to measure time.* Simon & Schuster.

Francis, M. (2014). Is this life real? *Aeon.* https://aeon.co/essays/is-reality-a-computer-simulation-does-it-matter

Fuchs, T. (2018). The cyclical time of the body and its relation to linear time. *Journal of Consciousness Studies, 25*(7–8), 47–65. https://www.ingentaconnect.com/contentone/imp/jcs/2018/00000025/f0020007/art00003

Galison, P. (2003). *Einstein's clocks, Poincaré's maps.* Sceptre.

Garfield, S. (2016). *Timekeepers.* Canongate.

Garrard, E., & Wrigley, A. (2009). Hope and terminal illness: False hope versus absolute hope. *Clinical Ethics, 4*, 38–43. https://doi.org/10.1258/ce.2008.008050

Giddens, A. (1990). *The consequences of modernity.* Polity Press.

Giddens, A. (1991). *Modernity and self-identity*. Polity Press.

Glennie, P., & Thrift, N. (2009). *Shaping the day*. Oxford University Press.

Gupta, A., Eisenhauer, E. A., & Booth, C. M. (2022). The time toxicity of cancer treatment. *Journal of Clinical Oncology*, *40*(15), 1611–1615. https://doi.org/10.1200/JCO.21.02810

Hajar, R. (2015). History of medicine timeline. *Heart Views*, *16*(1), 43–45. https://doi.org/10.4103/1995-705x.153008

Hancock, P. A., & Hancock, G. M. (2014). The effects of age, sex, body temperature, heart rate, and time of day on the perception of time in life. *Time & Society*, *23*(2), 195–211. https://doi.org/10.1177/0961463X13479187

Harkin, L. J., & Kuss, D. (2021). "My smartphone is an extension of myself": A holistic qualitative exploration of the impact of using a smartphone. *Psychology of Popular Media*, *10*(1), 28–38. https://doi.org/10.1037/ppm0000278

Hawking, S. (1988). *A brief history of time*. Bantam Books.

Healy, J. D. (2003). Excess winter mortality in Europe: A cross country analysis identifying key risk factors. *Journal of Epidemiology & Community Health*, *57*(10), 784–789. http://doi.org/10.1136/jech.57.10.784

Heidegger, M. (1962). *Being and time*. [Trans. Macquarrie, J. & Robinson, E.] Blackwell Publishing.

Henkin, D. (2021). *How we became weekly*. Aeon. https://aeon.co/essays/how-we-came-to-depend-on-the-week-despite-its-artificiality

Hernandez, W. A. (2016). St. Augustine on time. *International Journal of Humanities and Social Science*, *6*(6), 37–40. http://www.ijhssnet.com/journal/index/3525

Hess-Holden, C. L., Monaghan, C. L., & Justice, C. A. (2017). Pet bereavement support groups: A guide for mental health professionals. *Journal of Creativity in Mental Health*, *12*(4), 440–450. https://doi.org/10.1080/15401383.2017.1328291

Higgs, E. (2004). *Life, death and statistics*. Local Population Studies.

Hogue, D. A. (2006). Whose rite is it, anyway? Liminality and the work of the Christian funeral. *Liturgy*, *21*(1), 3–10. https://doi.org/10.1080/04580630500285949

Holford-Strevens, L. (2005). *The history of time a very short introduction*. Oxford University Press.

Honkasalo, M.-L. (2006). Fragilities in life and death: Engaging in uncertainty in modern society. *Health, Risk & Society*, *8*(1), 27–41. https://doi.org/10.1080/13698570500532355

Horner, R., & Carmody, P. (2020). *Global north/south* (2nd ed., Vol. 6, pp. 181–1870). International Encyclopedia of Human Geography. https://doi.org/10.1016/B978-0-08-102295-5.10648-1

Howarth, G. (2007). *Death & dying a sociological introduction*. Polity Press.

Hussey, K. D. (2021). 'The waste of daylight': Rhythmicity, workers' health and Britain's Edwardian daylight saving time bills. *Social History of Medicine*, *35*(2), 422–443. https://doi.org/10.1093/shm/hkab105

Hussey, K. (2022). *Timeless spaces: Cave experiments in chronobiology*. https://www.museion.ku.dk/2022/04/timeless-spaces-cave-experiments-in-chronobiology/

Impey, C. (2021). The most powerful space telescope ever built will look back in time to the Dark Ages of the universe. *The Conversation, Canada*. https://theconversation.com/the-most-powerful-space-telescope-ever-built-will-look-back-in-time-to-the-dark-ages-of-the-universe-169603

International Committee of the Red Cross. (2017). *Missing migrants and their families*. ICRC. https://www.icrc.org/en/publication/missing-migrants-and-their-families-icrcs-recommendations-policy-makers

International Criminal Court. (2011). *Rome statute of the International Criminal Court*. The Hague. https://www.un.org/en/genocideprevention/crimes-against-humanity.shtml

Janeja, M. K., & Bandak, A. (Eds.). (2018). *Ethnographies of waiting*. Bloomsbury Academic.

Johnson, S. (2007). Hope in terminal illness: An evolutionary concept analysis. *International Journal of Palliative Nursing*, *13*(9), 451–459. http://doi.org/10.12968/ijpn.2007.13.9.27418

Jones, I., & Quigley, M. (2016). Preventing lawful and decent burial: Resurrecting dead offences. *Legal Studies*, *36*(2), 354–374. https://doi.org/10.1111/lest.12117

de Jong, I. J. F. (2007). Introduction. Narratological theory on time. In I. J. F. de Jong & R. Nunlist (Eds.), *Time in Ancient Greek literature* (pp. 1–16). Brill.

Kasket, E. (2012). Continuing bonds in the age of social networking: Facebook as a modern-day medium. *Bereavement Care*, *31*(2), 62–69. https://doi.org/10.1080/02682621.2012.710493

Kasket, E. (2019). *All the ghosts in the machine: The digital afterlife of your personal data*. Robinson.

Kastenbaum, R. (1999). The moment of death: Is hospice making a difference? *The Hospice Journal*, *14*(3–4), 253–270. https://doi.org/10.1080/0742-969X.1999.11882943

Katz, O., & Greene, K. S. (2021). Constructing time in uncertainty: Temporal regimes among missing persons' families. *Current Sociology*, *69*(1), 59–76. https://doi.org/10.1177/0011392120902235

Kaufman-Scarborough, C., & Lindquist, J. D. (2003). Understanding the experience of time scarcity. *Time & Society*, *12*(2–3), 349–370. https://doi.org/10.1177/0961463X030122011

Kellehear, A. (2013). Vigils for the dying: Origin and functions of a persistent tradition. *Illness, Crisis, and Loss*, (21)2, 109–124. https://doi.org/10.2190/IL.21.2.c

Kellehear, A. (2014). *The inner life of the dying person*. Columbia University Press.

Kenny, K., Broom, A., Kirby, E., & Ridge, D. (2019). In one's own time: Contesting the temporality and linearity of bereavement. *Health*, *23*(1), 58–75. https://doi.org/10.1177/1363459317724854

Kirton-Darling, E. (2022). *Death, family and the law*. Bristol University Press.

Kitzinger, C., & Kitzinger, J. (2014). 'This in-between': How families talk about death in relation to severe brain injury and disorders of consciousness. In L. Van Brussel & N. Carpentier (Eds.), *The social construction of death* (pp. 239–258). Palgrave MacMillan.

Klass, D., & Steffen, E. M. (2018). Introduction – Continuing bonds 20 years on. In D. Klass & E. M. Steffen (Eds.), *Continuing bonds in bereavement* (pp. 1–14). Routledge.

Klein, S. (2007). *Time: A user's guide* [Trans. by Frisch, S.] Penguin Books.

Klinenberg, E. (2001). Dying alone. The social production of urban isolation. *Ethnography*, *2*(4), 501–531. https://doi.org/10.1177/14661380122231019

Koksvik, G. H. (2020). Neoliberalism, individual responsibilization and the death positivity movement. *International Journal of Cultural Studies, 23*(6), 951–967. https://doi.org/10.1177/1367877920924426

Králová, J. (2015). What is social death? *Contemporary Social Science, 10*(3), 235–248. https://doi.org/10.1080/21582041.2015.1114407

Kulakiewicz, A., & Balogun, B. (2021). *Public access to automatic External defibrillators.* House of Commons Library.

Kumaar, S. S. (2022). Chronology of calendar: Human evolution journey. *International Journal of History, 4*(1), 17–22. https://doi.org/10.22271/27069109.2022.v4.i1a.124

Kumar, S., Ali, W., Singh, U. S., Kumar, A., Bhattacharya, S., Verma, A. K., & Rupani, R. (2016). Temperature-dependent postmortem changes in human Cardiac Troponin-T (cTnT): An approach in estimation of time since death. *Journal of Forensic Sciences, 61*(S1). https://doi.org/10.1111/1556-4029.12928

Last, M. (2013). Dying on time: Cultures of death and time in Muslim Northern Nigeria. In D. E. Refslund & R. Willerslev (Eds.), *Taming time, timing death* (pp. 247–264). Routledge.

Lockwood, M. (2005). *The labyrinth of time.* Oxford University Press.

Lofland, L. H. (1978). *The craft of dying.* Sage.

Luckmann, T. (1991). The constitution of human life in time. In J. Bender & D. E. Wellbery (Eds.), *Chronotypes the construction of time* (pp. 151–166). Stanford University Press.

Luper, S. (2009). *The philosophy of death.* Cambridge University Press.

MacArtney, J. I., BroomKirby, A. E., Good, P., & Wootton, J. (2015). The liminal and the parallax: Living and dying at the end of life. *Qualitative Health Research, 27*(5), 623–633. https://doi.org/10.1177/1049732315618938

Madea, B. (Ed.). (2016). *Estimation of the time since death* (3rd ed.). CRC Press.

Majid, U., & Akande, A. (2022). Managing anticipatory grief in family and partners: A systematic review and qualitative meta-synthesis. *The Family Journal: Counseling and Therapy for Couples and Families, 30*(2), 242–249. https://doi.org/10.1177/10664807211000715

Margolis, H. (2018). A brief history of timekeeping. *Physics World, 31*(11), 27–30. https://physicsworld.com/a/a-brief-history-of-timekeeping/

Mathijssen, B. (2021). The human corpse as aesthetic-therapeutic. *Mortality, 28*(1), 37–53. https://doi.org/10.1080/13576275.2021.1876009

Matuszewski, S. (2021). Post-Mortem interval estimation based on insect evidence: Current challenges. *Insects, 12,* 314. https://doi.org/10.3390/insects12040314

Matz, J. (2012). J. B. Priestley in the theater of time. *Modernism/Modernity, 19*(2), 321–342. https://doi.org/10.1353/mod.2012.0040

Maugham, W. S. (1933/2017). Plays: Volume one. *Vintage.*

Maxwell, E. (2013). Would your records stand up to scrutiny? *Nursing Times.* https://www.nursingtimes.net/opinion/would-your-records-stand-up-to-scrutiny-13-09-2013/

May, T. (2009). *Death.* Acumen.

Menzies, R. E., & Menzies, R. G. (2021). *Mortals: How the Fear of death shaped human society.* Allen & Unwin.

Millares-Martin, P. (2020). Death certification in England must evolve (Considering current technology). *Journal of Forensic and Legal Medicine, 69*. https://doi.org/10.1016/j.jflm.2019.101882

Mills, C. W. (1959). *The sociological imagination*. Oxford University Press.

Ministry of Justice. (2022). *Coroner statistics 2021: England and Wales*. https://www.gov.uk/government/statistics/coroners-statistics-2021/coroners-statistics-2021-england-and-wales

Moon, C. (2016). Human rights, human remains: Forensic humanitarianism and the human rights of the dead. *International Social Science Journal, 65*(215–216), 49–63. https://doi.org/10.1111/issj.12071

Moon, C. (2019). What remains? Human rights after death. In K. Squires, D. Errickson, & N. Marquez-Grant (Eds.), *Ethical approaches to human remains* (pp. 39–58). Springer.

Moon, C. (2020). Extraordinary deathwork: New developments in, and the social significance of, forensic humanitarian action. In R. C. Parra, S. C. Zapico, & D. H. Ubelaker (Eds.), *Forensic science and humanitarian action: Interacting with the dead and the living* (pp. 37–48). John Wiley & Sons.

Mroz, S., Dierick, S., Deliens, L., Cohen, J., & Chambaere, K. (2020). Assisted dying around the world: A status quaestionis. *Annals of Palliative Medicine*. https://doi.org/10.21037/apm-20-637

Mulkay, M., & Ernst, J. (1991). The changing profile of social death. *European Journal of Sociology, 32*, 172–196. https://doi.org/10.1017/S0003975600006214

Nail, T. (2022). What is the philosophy of movement? *Mobility Humanities, 1*(1), 9–25. https://journal-mobilityhumanities.com/archives/?ckattempt=1&mod=document&uid=27

National Medical Examiner. (2023). *The national medical examiner's report 2022*. NHS England and NHS Improvement. https://www.england.nhs.uk/publication/national-medical-examiner-reports/

Neimeyer, R. A., Klass, D., & Dennis, M. R. (2014). A social constructionist account of grief: Loss and the narration of meaning. *Death Studies, 38*(8), 485–498. https://doi.org/10.1080/07481187.2014.913454

Nielsen, K., & Skotnicki, T. (2019). Sociology towards death: Heidegger, time and social theory. *Journal of Classical Sociology, 19*(2), 111–137. https://doi.org/10.1177/1468795X1877274

Nowotny, H. (1994). *Time: The modern and postmodern experience* [Trans. N. Plaice]. Polity Press.

Nuffield Trust. (2022, May 4). Cancer waiting times. https://www.nuffieldtrust.org.uk/resource/cancer-waiting-time-targets#background

Office for National Statistics. (2008). *Guidance for doctors completing medical certificates of cause of death in England and Wales*. https://www.gov.uk/government/publications/guidance-notes-for-completing-a-medical-certificate-of-cause-of-death

Office for National Statistics. (2014). *Mortality in the United Kingdom: 1983–2013*. https://www.ons.gov.uk/peoplepopulationandcommunity/birthsdeathsandmarriages/deaths/articles/mortalityintheunitedkingdom/19832013

Office for National Statistics. (2021). *User guide to mortality statistics*. https://www.ons.gov.uk/peoplepopulationandcommunity/birthsdeathsandmarriages/deaths/methodologies/userguidetomortalitystatisticsjuly2017

Office for National Statistics. (2022a). *Deaths of homeless people in England and Wales: 2021 registrations.* https://www.ons.gov.uk/peoplepopulationandco mmunity/birthsdeathsandmarriages/deaths/bulletins/deathsofhomelesspeoplei nenglandandwales/2021registrations

Office for National Statistics. (2022b). *Deaths registered in England and Wales: 2021.* https://www.ons.gov.uk/peoplepopulationandcommunity/birthsdeathsandmarria ges/deaths/bulletins/deathsregistrationsummarytables/2021

Office for National Statistics. (2022c). *Monthly mortality analysis, England and Wales: May 2022.* https://www.ons.gov.uk/peoplepopulationandcommunity/birthsdeaths andmarriages/deaths/bulletins/monthlymortalityanalysisenglandandwales/ may2022

Office for National Statistics. (2023). *Child and infant mortality in England and Wales: 2021.* https://www.ons.gov.uk/peoplepopulationandcommunity/birthsdeathsand marriages/deaths/bulletins/childhoodinfantandperinatalmortalityinenglandand wales/2021

Ogden, R. S., Dobbins, C., Slade, K., McIntyre, J., & Fairclough, S. (2022). The psychophysiological mechanisms of real-world time experience. *Nature Scientific Reports, 12*(12890). https://doi.org/10.1038/s41598-022-16198-z

Park, C. L. (2021). The meaning of beliefs in communicating with god and the deceased for individuals' well-being. In T. G. Plante & G. E. Schwartz (Eds.), *Human interaction with the divine, the sacred, and the deceased* (pp. 234–244). Taylor & Francis.

Parsons, B. (2017). Premature burial and the undertakers. In S. McCorristine (Ed.), *Interdisciplinary perspectives on mortality and its timings* (pp. 69–85). Palgrave Historical Studies in the Criminal Corpse and its Afterlife. https://doi.org/ 10.1057/978-1-137-58328-4_5

Pasveer, B. (2019). Deadlines: Doing times in (Dutch) hospice. *Mortality, 24*(3), 319–332. https://doi.org/10.1080/13576275.2018.1461817

Patel, P., & Quilter-Pinner, H. (2022). *The road to renewal: Elections, parties and the case for renewing democracy.* Institute for Public Policy Research. https:// www.ippr.org/research/publications/road-to-renewal

Prior, L. (1985). Making sense of mortality. *Sociology of Health & Illness, 7*(2), 167–190. https://doi.org/10.1111/1467-9566.ep10949063

Prior, L. (1989). *The social organization of death.* MacMillan.

Rée, J. (2017). The last moment. In S. McCorristine (Ed.), *Interdisciplinary perspectives on mortality and its timings.* Palgrave Historical Studies in the Criminal Corpse and its Afterlife (pp. 133–144). https://doi.org/10.1057/978-1- 137-58328-4_5

Reith, M., & Payne, M. (2009). *Social work in end-of-life and palliative care.* Policy Press.

Richards, E. G. (1998). *Mapping time.* Oxford University Press.

Richards, N. (2017). Assisted suicide as a remedy for suffering? The end-of-life preferences of British "Suicide Tourists". *Medical Anthropology, 36*(4), 348–362. http://doi.org/10.1080/01459740.2016.1255610

Ritchie, H., Spooner, F., & Roser, M. (2019). *Causes of death.* Our World in Data. https://ourworldindata.org/causes-of-death

Roser, M. (2021). *Causes of death globally: What do people die from?* Our World in Data. https://ourworldindata.org/causes-of-death-treemap

Roux-Kemp, A. (2008). The moment of death: Law, science and society. *Obiter, 29*(2), 260–267. https://ssrn.com/abstract=2441448

Rovelli, C. (2017). *The order of time* [Trans. E. Segre & S. Carnel] Penguin Books.

Rovers, J. J. E., Knol, E. J., Pieksma, J., Nienhuis, W., Wichmann, A. B., & Engels, Y. (2019). Living at the end-of-life: Experience of time of patients with cancer. *BMC Palliative Care, 18*(40). https://doi.org/10.1186/s12904-019-0424-7

Rugg, J., & Jones, S. (2019). *Funeral experts by experience: What matters to them*. The University of York. https://eprints.whiterose.ac.uk/162914/

Rynasiewicz, R. (2022). Newton's views on space, time, and motion. In N. Zalta (Ed.), *The Stanford encyclopedia of philosophy*. https://plato.stanford.edu/archives/spr2022/entries/newton-stm/

Sachs, J. S. (2001). *Corpse*. Basic Books.

Sacks, O. (2015). *On the move: A life*. Picador.

Sacks, J. L., & Nelson, J. P. (2007). A theory of nonphysical suffering and trust in hospice patients. *Qualitative Health Research, 17*(5), 675–689. https://doi.org/10.1177/1049732306298524

Salisbury, H. (2022). Death – The great leveller? *British Medical Journal, 378*. http://doi.org/10.1136/bmj.o2202

Sandberg, E. (2022). Under the net: Universal time, modernism, and the subversive temporality of golden age detective fiction. *Textual Practice*. https://doi.org/10.1080/0950236X.2022.2148729

Savin-Baden, M. (2019). Postdigital afterlife? *Postdigital Science and Education, 1*, 303–306. https://doi.org/10.1007/s42438-019-00056-9

Sayer, D. (2010). Who's afraid of the dead? Archaeology, modernity and the death taboo. *World Archaeology, 42*(3), 481–491. https://doi.org/10.1080/00438243.2010.498665

Schick, A. (2022). Health as temporally extended: Theoretical foundations and implications. *History & Philosophy of the Life Sciences, 44*(32). https://doi.org/10.1007/s40656-022-00513-y

Schweizer, H. (2008). *On waiting*. Routledge.

Seale, C. (1998). *Constructing death: The sociology of dying and bereavement*. Cambridge University Press.

Shakespeare, W. (1604). The tragedy of Othello, the Moor of Venice. W. Shakespeare (Ed.), The complete works. Based on the 1974 Riverside Edition. Kobo Edition.

Shaw, M. (2012). Sociology and genocide. In D. Bloxham & A. D. Moses (Eds.), *The Oxford handbook of genocide studies* (pp. 142–162). Oxford University Press.

Shpancer, N. (2020). *Our memories, ourselves*. Psychology Today. https://www.psychologytoday.com/us/blog/insight-therapy/202001/our-memories-ourselves

Shrestha, R., Kanchan, T., & Krishan, K. (2021). *Methods of estimation of time since death*. StatPearls: Internet. https://www.ncbi.nlm.nih.gov/books/NBK549867/

Sibbens, L., Van de Voorde, W., Decarte, R., & Bekaert, B. (2017). The development of a forensic clock to determine time of death. *Forensic Science International: Genetics Supplement Series*. http://doi.org/10.1016/j.fsigss.2017.09.059

Silverman, G. S., Baroiller, A., & Hemer, S. R. (2021). Culture and grief: Ethnographic perspectives on ritual, relationships and remembering. *Death Studies, 45*(1), 1–8. https://doi.org/10.1080/07481187.2020.1851885

Smart, B. (2002). *Michel Foucault* (2nd ed.). Routledge.

Smith, M., Dominguez-Gil, B., Greer, D. M., Manara, A. R., & Souter, M. J. (2019). Organ donation after circulatory death: Current status and future potential. *Intensive Care Medicine, 45*, 310–321. https://doi.org/10.1007/s00134-019-05533-0

Sobel, D. (1995). *Longitude*. Fourth Estate.

Strawson, G. (2015). *I am not a story*. Aeon Essays. https://aeon.co/essays/let-s-ditch-the-dangerous-idea-that-life-is-a-story

Sudnow, D. (1967). *Passing on: The social organization of dying*. Prentice-Hall.

Tallis, R. (2016). Time & change. *Philosophy Now, 115*. https://philosophynow.org/issues/115/Time_and_Change

Terunuma, Y., & Mathis, B. J. (2021). Cultural sensitivity in brain death determination: A necessity in end-of-life decisions in Japan. *BMC Medical Ethics, 22*(58). https://doi.org/10.1186/s12910-021-00626-2

Timmons, S., Crosbie, B., & Harrison-Paul, R. (2010). Displacement of death in public space by lay people using the automated external defibrillator. *Health & Place, 16*, 365–370. https://doi.org/10.1016/j.healthplace.2009.11.008

Tomasini, F. (2017). *Remembering and disremembering the dead*. Palgrave Historical Studies in the Criminal Corpse and its Afterlife. Palgrave MacMillan. https://doi.org/10.1057/978-1-137-53828-4_2

Topham, G. (2022, June 30). Ministers unveil plan to tackle airport crisis after fresh Heathrow disruption. *The Guardian*. https://www.theguardian.com/uk-news/2022/jun/30/heathrow-passengers-flights-cancelled-airlines

Turner, V. (1969). *The ritual process: Structure and anti-structure*. Aldine Transaction.

Turner, B. S. (2022). Vulnerability and existence theory in catastrophic times. *Journal of Classical Sociology, 22*(1), 90–94. https://doi.org/10.1177/1468795X211049303

Turner, N., & Caswell, G. (2020). Moral ambiguity in media reports of dying alone. *Mortality, 25*(3), 266–281. https://doi.org/10.1080/13576275.2019.1657388

Turner, N., & Caswell, G. (2022). A relative absence: Exploring professional experiences of funerals without mourners. *Omega: The Journal of Death and Dying, 85*(4), 868–886. https://journals.sagepub.com/doi/full/10.1177/0030222820959960

UK Parliament. (2014). *Recording and registering death*. https://www.parliament.uk/about/living-heritage/transformingsociety/private-lives/death-dying/dying-and-death/registeringdeath/

University of Melbourne. (2016). *Improving cause of death information*. https://crvsgateway.info/The-International-Form-of-Medical-Certificate-of-Cause-of-Death~356

Vagni, G. (2022). From me to you: Time together and subjective well-being in the UK. *Sociology, 56*(2), 262–279. https://doi.org/10.1177/00380385211033147

Valentine, C. (2007). The "moment of death". *Omega, 55*(3), 219–236. https://doi.org/10.2190/OM.55.3.d

Valentine, C. (2013). Identity and post-mortem relationships in the narratives of British and Japanese mourners. *The Sociological Review, 61*, 383–401. https://doi.org/10.1111/1467-954X.12022

Van Cauter, E., & Turek, F. W. (1986). Depression: A disorder of timekeeping? *Perspectives in Biology and Medicine, 29*(4), 510–520. https://doi.org/10.1353/pbm.1986.0033

Van Gennep, A. (1909). *The rites of passage*. Routledge & Kegan Paul.

Van Kleef, G. A., Cheshin, A., Fischer, A. H., & Schneider, K. (2016). Editorial: The social nature of emotions. *Frontiers in Psychology*. https://doi.org/10.3389/fpsyg.2016.00896

Van Schaik, T., & Wojtkowiak, J. (2022). Disembodied ritual: An explorative study on the meanings of physical absence during funerals by bereaved in times of COVID-19. *Death Studies*, *47*(7), 873–880. https://doi.org/10.1080/07481187.2022.2135047

Voas, D., & Bruce, S. (2019). *British social attitudes: 36 religion*. The National Centre for Social Research. https://bsa.natcen.ac.uk/latest-report/british-social-attitudes-36/key-findings.aspx

Walter, T. (1991). Modern death: Taboo or not taboo? *Sociology*, *25*(2), 293–310. https://doi.org/10.1177/0038038591025002009

Walter, T. (1999). *On bereavement*. Open University Press.

Watson, K. D. (2011). *Forensic medicine in western society a history*. Routledge.

Webb, W. A., Mitchell, T., Snelling, P., & Nyatanga, B. (2020). Life's hard and then you die: The end-of-life priorities of people experiencing homelessness in the UK. *International Journal of Palliative Nursing*, *26*(3), 120–132. https://doi.org/10.12968/ijpn.2020.26.3.120

Wells, H. G. (1895/2005). *The time machine*. Penguin Classics.

Wels, H., van der Waalk, Spiegel, A., & Kamsteeg, F. (2011). Victor Turner and liminality: An introduction. *Anthropology Southern Africa*, *34*(1&2), 1–4. https://doi.org/10.1080/23323256.2011.11500002

Westcott, D. J. (2018). Recent advances in forensic anthropology: Decomposition research. *Forensic Sciences Research*, *3*(4), 278–293. https://doi.org/10.1080/20961790.2018.1488571

White, N., Reid, F., Harris, A., Harries, P., & Stone, P. (2016). A systematic review of predictions of survival in palliative care: How accurate are clinicians and who are the experts? *PLoS One*, *11*(8), e0161407. https://doi.org/10.1371/journal.pone.0161407

Widlok, T., Knab, J., & van der Wulp, C. (2020). #African time: Making the future legible. *African Studies*, *80*(3–4), 397–414. https://doi.org/10.1080/00020184.2021.1942786

Williams, T., & Pfeiffer, D. (2017). Unpacking the mind of evil: A sociological perspective on the role of intent and motivations in genocide. *Genocide Studies and Prevention: International Journal*, *11*(2), 72–87. http://doi.org/10.5038/1911-9933.11.2.1485

Wilson, J., Laverty, D., & Cooper, M. (2019). *Of care after death: Registered Nurse Verification of Expected Adult Death (RNVoEAD) guidance* (2nd ed.). Hospice UK.

Woodthorpe, K. (2017). Family and funerals: Taking a relational perspective. *Death Studies*, *41*(9), 592–601. https://doi.org/10.1080/07481187.2017.1325419

World Health Organization. (2014). Civil registration: Why counting births and deaths is important. https://www.who.int/news-room/fact-sheets/detail/civil-registration-why-counting-births-and-deaths-is-important

World Health Organization. (2020). *The top ten causes of death*. https://www.who.int/news-room/fact-sheets/detail/the-top-10-causes-of-death

World Health Organization. (2021). *International classification of diseases – 11 for mortality and morbidity statistics*. https://icd.who.int/browse11/l-m/en#/http%3a%2f%2fid.who.int%2ficd%2fentity%2f1876291018

World Health Organization. (2023a). *International statistical classification of diseases and related health problems (ICD).* https://www.who.int/standards/classifications/classification-of-diseases

World Health Organization. (2023b). *Cause of death on the death certificate: Quick reference guide.* https://www.who.int/standards/classifications/classification-of-diseases/cause-of-death

Yates, K. (2019). The maths of life and death. *Quercus.*

Yin, R. K. (2009). *Case study research* (4th ed.). Sage.

Young, N. (2022). Agents of change: Temporal flow and feeling oneself act. *Philosophical Studies, 179,* 2619–2637. https://doi.org/10.1007/s11098-022-01790-w

Zeng, X., Adair, T., Wang, L., Yin, P., Qi, J., Liu, Y., Liu, J., Lopez, A. D., & Zhou, M. (2020). Measuring the completeness of death registration in 2844 Chinese counties in 2018. *BMC Medicine, 18*(176). https://doi.org/10.1186/s12916-020-01632-8

Zerubavel, E. (1981). *Hidden rhythms.* University of California Press.

Zigon, J. (2018). Hope and waiting in post-Soviet Moscow. In M. K. Janeja & A. Bandak (Eds.), *Ethnographies of waiting.* Bloomsbury Academic.

Zilg, B., Bernard, S., Alkass, K., Berg, S., & Druid, H. (2015). A new model for the estimation of time of death from vitreous potassium levels corrected for age and temperature. *Forensic Science International, 254,* 158–166. http://doi.org/10.1016/j.forsciint.2015.07.020

Zivkovic, T. (2018). Forecasting and foreclosing futures: The temporal dissonance of advance care directives. *Social Science & Medicine, 215,* 16–22. https://doi.org/10.1016/j.socscimed.2018.08.035

Index